Quantum Cryptography in Advanced Networks

Edited by Oleg G. Morozov

Published in London, United Kingdom

IntechOpen

Supporting open minds since 2005

Quantum Cryptography in Advanced Networks
http://dx.doi.org/10.5772/intechopen.75258
Edited by Oleg G. Morozov

Contributors
Yongli Zhao, Josue Lopez-Leyva, Ariana Talamantes-Alvarez, Miguel Ponce-Camacho, Eduardo Alvarez-Guzman, Edith Garcia, Nicolae Enaki, Oleg Morozov

Notice
Statements and opinions expressed in the chapters are these of the individual contributors and not necessarily those of the editors or publisher. No responsibility is accepted for the accuracy of information contained in the published chapters. The publisher assumes no responsibility for any damage or injury to persons or property arising out of the use of any materials, instructions, methods or ideas contained in the book.

First published in London, United Kingdom, 2019 by IntechOpen
IntechOpen is the global imprint of INTECHOPEN LIMITED, registered in England and Wales, registration number: 11086078, The Shard, 25th floor, 32 London Bridge Street
London, SE19SG – United Kingdom
Printed in Croatia

British Library Cataloguing-in-Publication Data
A catalogue record for this book is available from the British Library

Additional hard and PDF copies can be obtained from orders@intechopen.com

Quantum Cryptography in Advanced Networks
Edited by Oleg G. Morozov
p. cm.
Print ISBN 978-1-83962-249-6
Online ISBN 978-1-83962-250-2
eBook (PDF) ISBN 978-1-83962-251-9

Meet the editor

Oleg G. Morozov is full professor of Kazan National Research Technical University n.a. Andrey Tupolev (KNRTU-KAI), Head of Radiophotonics and Microwave Technologies Department, and Director of R&D Institute of Applied Electrodynamics, Photonics and Living Systems. He leads research on microwave photonics, fiber optic sensors and communications, and transfer of optical methods into microwave sensors and technologies. He has over 100 papers and 10 monographs concerning the principles of tandem amplitude-phase modulation of microwave and optical carriers, and its application in the wide spectrum of technical and living systems. Over the past five years, his interests have been in the field of quantum communications, in particular, the quantum key distribution of frequency-coded subcarriers. Research in this area is carried out jointly with the Kazan Quantum Center of KNRTU-KAI. Oleg G. Morozov is an Honorary Worker of Higher Education, Fellow of the International Academy of Telecommunications, Senior Member of OSA and SPIE, and regular member of the Optical Society n.a. Rojdestvenskiy (ROS), EOS, and IEEE.

Contents

Preface

Quantum cryptography (QC) is a special powerful tool for the wide spectrum of security applications based on both fundamental and applied principles of quantum mechanics, which allows two subscribers to generate, exchange, and process perfectly unique keys via a potentially insecure and intercepting quantum channel. Proposed 35 years ago, quantum key distribution (QKD), as a process to realize the advantages of QC, attracts more and more attention. Significant progress has been made in both its theory and practice from many points of view. The present book has four exclusive chapters. All chapters are focused on the most important provable developments in this critically important area of humankind wide spectra communications, because transferring information in a secure and private manner is a key ingredient to many aspects of society.

QKD systems with carrier modulation coding are prominent representatives of classical fiber telecommunication systems based on the principles of microwave photonics, with their inherent advantages and disadvantages. If the former can be attributed to the universality of modulation schemes, and the undoubted provision of a high signal-to-noise ratio in both quantum and synchronization channels of almost any length, the latter will begin to manifest with a constant increase in the range of quantum communication channels and the duration of the connection. First of all, they should include polarization distortion and chromatic dispersion. The introductory chapter focuses on monitoring the chromatic dispersion of the synchronization channel, which is controlled by the same generators as Alice and Bob's quantum channels, but in the absence of phase switching corresponding to the polarization state of the photons. In particular, the monitoring of chromatic dispersion in the synchronization channel is considered with the possibility of eliminating the influence of polarization distortions and using a clock frequency equal to the phase switching frequency, with its separation in a fiber Bragg grating filter.

Optical network security is attracting increasing research interest. Currently, a software-defined optical network (SDON) has been proposed to increase network intelligence (e.g., flexibility and programmability), which is gradually moving towards industrialization. However, varieties of new threats are emerging in SDONs. Data encryption is an effective way to secure communications in SDONs. In the first chapter of the book "Quantum Key Distribution over Software Defined Optical Networks," an architecture of QKD over SDONs, based on the QKD enabling technologies, is presented. The resource allocation problem is elaborated in detail and is classified into wavelength allocation, time-slot allocation, and secret-key allocation problems in QKD over SDONs. Finally, several open issues and challenges are discussed.

Free-Space Optical Quantum Key Distribution (FSO-QKD) systems present an innovative way for sharing secure information between two parties located at ground stations, spacecraft, or aircraft. However, these scenarios present several challenges regarding the hardware, protocols, and techniques used that must be solved to enhance the performance parameters (security level, distance link, final secret key rate, among others) for any QKD system; although, in particular, a high transmission performance is required for both the classical and quantum channels. These issues impose the roadmap and trends in the research, academic, and manufacturing sectors around the world, which are presented and discussed in the second chapter of the book "Free-Space-Optical Quantum Key Distribution Systems: Challenges and Trends."

The third chapter "Coherence Proprieties of Entangled Bi-photon Fields and Its Application in Holography and Communication" is dedicated to the problem of coherence that appears not only between quanta, but between groups of photons, generated in the process of nonlinear interaction of an electromagnetic field with radiators. Two-photon interactions of light are today one of the main areas of research in quantum optics. The encrypted information, using the coherence of multi-mode bimodal field in quantum holography, opens a new perspective, in which the coherence proprieties between bi-photons are used together with non-local states of entangled photon pairs. This method of recording of information affords the new perspectives in QC, QKD, and quantum theory of information and opens new possibilities in the coding and decoding of data generally.

The editor is grateful to all the authors of the chapters for participating in the preparation of the book and hopes that its original material will undoubtedly benefit researchers, engineers, graduates, and doctoral students working in quantum cryptography and information security-related areas.

Oleg G. Morozov
Professor,
Radiophotonics and Microwave Technologies Department,
Institute of Radio Electronics and Telecommunications,
Kazan National Research Technical University,
named after A.N. Tupolev-KAI (KNRTU-KAI),
Kazan, Russia

Introductory Chapter: Chromatic Dispersion Monitoring in Synchronization Channel of Quantum Key Distribution Systems with Carrier Modulation Coding

Oleg G. Morozov

1. Introduction

The method of quantum key distribution (QKD) with carrier modulation coding (CMC) was proposed in [1, 2] and developed in [3–8]. Its advantages are the ease of input and coordination of the optical phase, the high data transfer rate, the fundamental possibility of frequency multiplexing of the signal, as well as the simplicity of constructing a consistent scheme. The main difference lies in the fact that in the QKD-CMC systems, the quantum signal is not generated directly by the source but is carried to side frequencies as a result of phase, amplitude modulation, or a combination of these. In the latter works, to each state of the photons, instead of the amplitude or phase of the modulating signal at a certain frequency, one or more lateral component frequencies either photon optical carrier [9, 10] are put into line. We in [11–13] present a universal system capable of realizing all the mentioned types of modulation transformation and the new one based on tandem amplitude modulation and phase commutation with partially or full suppressed carrier.

Alice and Bob's synchronization channel provides frequency and phase matching of the modulating signals. The deviation of the phase of the modulating signal from the base position during the re-modulation of the signal spectrum at Bob leads to a change in the radiation power at the side frequencies. A phase setting error, at the same time, reduces the visibility of the interference pattern and increases the level of quantum bit errors in the signal. The values of the optical signal-to-noise ratio (OSNR) in the system are also determined by the accuracy of setting the amplitude of the modulating signals of Alice and Bob.

The changing ambient temperature and chromatic dispersion (CD), in turn, depending on temperature, introduce an additional time-varying phase delay of the synchronization signal, which leads to a phase mismatch. In [14] it is shown that the correction of the clock phase should be carried out every 2–3 seconds to eliminate the influence of temperature and 2–3 hours to correct the effect of CD. If we take into account that CD itself can change both with a change in the temperature of the fiber and with a change in its configuration, we should speak about the need for its constant monitoring.

Problems of maintaining the phase and amplitude in the synchronization channel arose in the author's Microwave Photonics Lab., KNRTU-KAI, Kazan, when trying to create a QKD-CMC system model on a fiber wound on a reel and connected in a total length of 24 km. Similar problems have arisen for our colleagues from ITMO, Saint-Petersburg, and the Kazan Quantum Center, KNRTU-KAI, Kazan, when they built quantum systems at distances of several kilometers of the real network of JSC "Tattelecom" operator, Kazan. However, 100 km is the limit that is not yet successfully overcome. At greater distances, individual photons are simply absorbed by the fiber-optic transmission medium. The main problem for long-haul quantum cryptography is loss. It should be noted that today the project of the longest in Russia Kazan-Chistopol line, which is 160 km long, is being created at ITMO and KNRTU-KAI, which will undoubtedly face the problem of monitoring chromatic dispersion.

Due to the natural symmetry of modulated coding and the highest achievable ratio of the modulation conversions, amplitude-phase modulation with complete or partial suppression of the optical carrier has found a particularly wide application in the systems of microwave photonics [15–22]. Let us apply results of given papers and microwave photonic principals [23, 24] to design CD monitoring principles for synchronization channel of QKD-CMC systems.

We'll present the results of the radio-frequency clock signal (RFCS) method, chosen by us as the most simple in implementation and promising, for CD monitoring in high-speed and extended communication channels. The basic measurement error is determined by the level of variation of the laser power and the polarization-mode dispersion (PMD). The last successful implementation of the RFCS method uses the built-in Bragg notch filter (BNF) on the carrier frequency and calculating the ratio of the RFCS powers in the filtered and unfiltered branches of the measurement channel. It made possible to achieve CD measurements in the range from 0 to 200 pm/ns and increase their sensitivity to 0.12 dB/(ps/nm) regardless of the PMD presence [25].

However, the stability of the central wavelength of the BNF position, due to the change in environmental parameters, and the noise characteristics of the synchronization channel, became a significant influence on its results. For dynamic range of CD measurements near 30 dB, the error from the instability of the central BNF wavelength is ±1.5 dB, when a temperature change is ±1°C. It is also shown in [25] that the monitoring scheme becomes inoperable, when OSNR of measurements is less than 15 dB.

The main chapter is based on the materials of Morozov et al. (2010–2018) papers [11, 15–22] and additional and new results of theoretical and experimental researches in QKD-CMC theme [12, 13], so as direct [26] and miscellaneous applications [27–30]. The next chapter sections are organized as follows. The second section shows the poly-harmonic principles of BNF position central wavelength monitoring. The third section discusses OSNR gain determination in different cases of poly-harmonic probing. In conclusion, the received results are analyzed, and the key development challenges for CD monitoring in synchronization channel are highlighted.

2. Poly-harmonic principles of BNF central wavelength monitoring

In this section, we propose a microwave photonic method for monitoring CD in synchronization channel based on analysis of the BNF reflectance spectrum position. As the prototype of the CD measurement system, the methods described in [25, 26] were taken. A monitoring subchannel based on the analysis of the optical carrier signal reflected from the BNF was included in the method operation sequence. Before reflection, carrier of synchronization channel of QKD-CMC system is modulated by amplitude at the fCL/100 frequency in the data generation stage, where fCL is the frequency of the clock synchronization signal (1–10 GHz). The presence of modulated components allows probing the position of the BNF, tuned by the center to the optical carrier, and produces a mismatch signal for its detuning, in analogy with the microwave photonic method of FBG interrogation, presented by us in [27]. In the given paper, symmetrical two-frequency probing signal was used. We additionally consider the methods of amplitude-unbalanced three-frequency and symmetrical four-frequency probing. In [26] the possibility of OSNR increasing till 10–12 dB, when signal processing realized on frequency-modulated components beating envelope, was shown also for full telecommunication channel. We shall reanalyze these results from the point of our task view. We defined the parameters, which could be used for registration in monitoring system, and carried information about interaction between double-, three-, and four-frequency probing oscillations and BNF.

2.1 Two-frequency symmetrical probing

Symmetric double-frequency probing radiation is a complex signal with amplitude and phase modulation. The main feature of this signal is that all of its components (instantaneous envelope $A(t)$, phase $\theta(t)$, and frequency $\omega(t)$) depend on its component amplitude ratio A_1, A_2. We evaluated the modulation rate of double-frequency signal. Thereto we will use the modulation coefficient:

$$m = 2(A_{max} - A_{min})/2(A_{max} + A_{min}), \qquad (1)$$

where A_{max} is sum of A_1 and A_2, and A_{min} is its difference.

Calculation results for $m(\delta)$, where δ is referenced BNF detuning, are shown in **Figure 1** for different (A_1/A_2).

We also defined the phase gradient of double-frequency signal under it components amplitude changing. Calculation results of $\theta(\delta)$ are shown in **Figure 2** for different (A_1/A_2).

Analysis of the dependences $m(\delta)$ and $\theta(\delta)$ allows determination of BNF central wavelength shift, according to δ, during the measurement of modulation index m and phase θ of probing signal components A_1 and A_2 beating envelope.

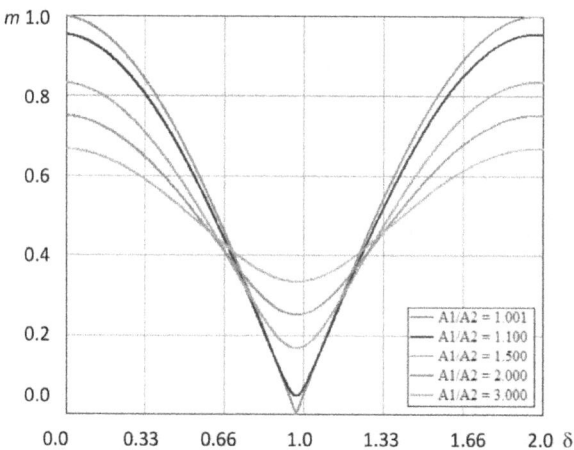

Figure 1.
Dependence $m(\delta)$ for different (A_1/A_2).

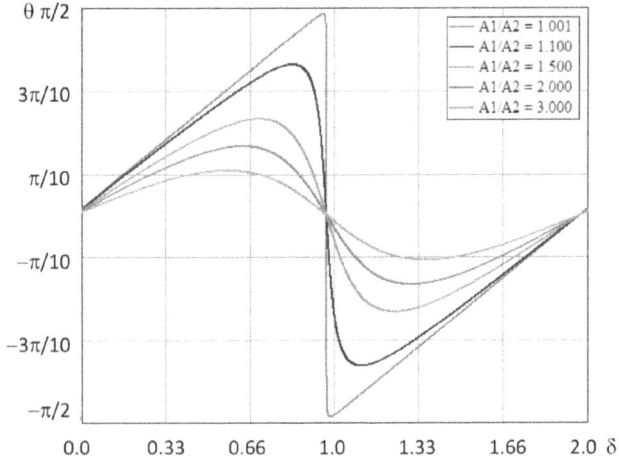

Figure 2.
Phase shift dependence $\theta(\delta)$ on component amplitude ratio A_1/A_2.

Produced on amplitude modulation coefficient or phase changing mismatch signals use to make correction in CD monitoring process or retuning the center wavelength of BNF.

2.2 Three-frequency symmetrical amplitude-unbalanced probing

It is known from a number of works that two-frequency probing, as simplest, does not always allow one to unambiguously determine the direction and magnitude of the BNF central wavelength shift from the wavelength of the carrier [28, 29]. Let us set the task of determining the position of the BNF central wavelength based on a three-frequency amplitude-unbalanced probing, relying only on the data coming from the photodetector PD to the ADC. Without changing the position of the carrier frequency of the probing radiation, we will shift the BNF in the range. For each position of the BNF, we analyze the parameters of the low-frequency signal at the output of the photodetector, tuned to determine the amplitude of the oscillations at the direct current (DC), the probing frequency fCL/100, and the doubled frequency 2fCL/100. The characteristics of the reflected signal level calculated from the three-frequency probing procedure on DC, 100 and 200 MGz for the central frequency position and detuning, are shown in **Figure 3**.

Taking into account the position of the BNF relative to the carrier, we can say analogically [31] that we reduce the error in the CD measurement by 10% (3 dB).

2.3 Four-frequency symmetrical probing

Two pairs of probing signals shifted from the carrier are sent to the mediums of the left and right slopes of BNF. Bragg wavelength of BNF is equal to the carrier wavelength; different frequency inside pair is equal to 100 MHz. The outputs of photodetector signals are formed, corresponding to the beating of the first (channel 1) and second (channel 2) signal pairs [20, 30]. By measuring the difference between amplitudes of each beating envelope, one can unambiguously determine detuning sign and value of central BNF wavelength.

Three cases of DNF deviation are shown in **Figure 4**.

In the first point, the BNF offset from the resonance wavelength is absent, and the output amplitudes of beating envelopes are equal.

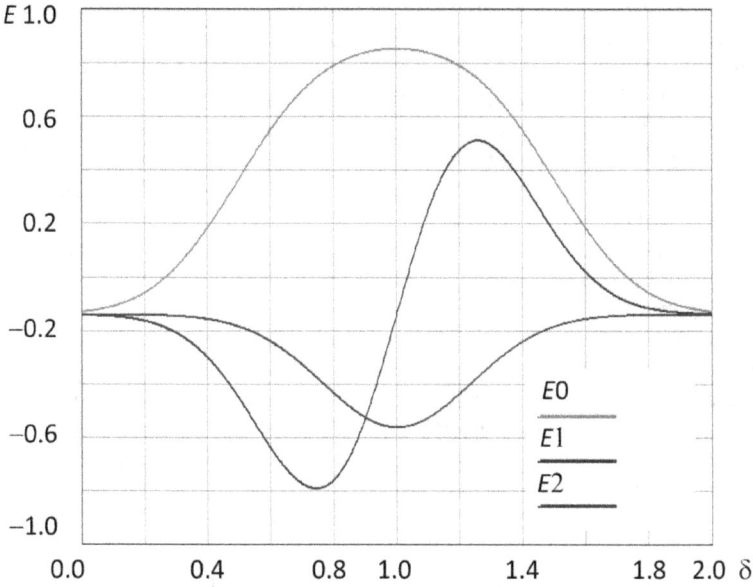

Figure 3.
Components reflected from BNF and their levels calculated for the three-frequency probing radiation at central (carrier) position and its detuning.

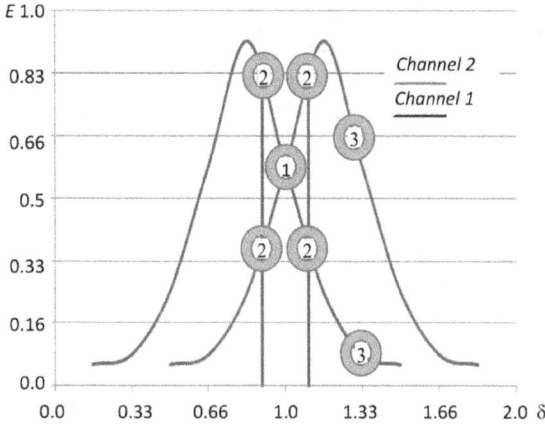

Figure 4.
Three cases of BNF deviation for four-frequency method.

In the second point, there is a slight BNF deviation, and the direction and magnitude of the deviation are determined by greater amplitude of beating envelopes.

In the third point, there is a significant deviation, and the direction and magnitude of the deviation are determined by the presence of a signal of beating envelopes and its level in one of the channels.

3. OSNR problem for CD monitoring in synchronization channel

For experimental part, we chose three-frequency method, as less compliant in comparison with four-frequency one. The procedure for monitoring the position of the BNF in synchronization channel can be implemented to RFCS method realization structure. In this case, it contains one narrowband photodetector with a 10 GHz band and filters tuned to frequencies at 0, 100 and 200 MHz from the carrier with a bandwidth of 10 MHz. The procedure for such analysis relates to in-line monitoring procedures, and the arrangement of frequency components at a frequency of 100 MHz from the frequency of the RFCS allows us to speak about identical for all three constituent CD parameters and the corresponding identical change in their amplitudes as it increases or decreases.

Using the algorithm for approximating BNF spectrum by the Gaussian curve at each measurement makes it possible to increase the accuracy of determining its central wavelength by an order.

Without going into the details of the physical nature of the phenomena, the level of the main noise of the photodetectors is higher than the level of background noise of scattering in the fiber and elements of the installation and determines the possibility of detecting the received signal (**Figure 5**). The gain in improving the OSNR in comparison with single-frequency measurements on the RFCS is determined by the following expression [15–20, 27]:

$$G = \left[\int_0^{BW_{PD}} S \right] \Big/ \left[\int_0^{BW_3} S + \int_{\frac{f_{CL}}{100} - \frac{BW_3}{2}}^{\frac{f_{CL}}{100} + \frac{BW_3}{2}} S + \int_{\frac{2f_{CL}}{100} - \frac{BW_3}{2}}^{\frac{2f_{CL}}{100} + \frac{BW_3}{2}} S \right], \qquad (2)$$

where $S = S(f)df$ is the spectral noise density of the receiver, BW_{PD} is the bandwidth of the PD equal to 10 GHz, and BW_3 is the frequency band of filters (10 MHz) at frequencies of 0, 100–200 MHz.

The gain is determined by the different filter bandwidth, nature, and noise level in different frequency regions $S(f)$ for different types of photodetector (with bandwidths 10 GHz) and filters (with bandwidths 10 MHz), respectively. In filter regions near 100 and 200 MHz, there are only thermal and shot noises. Current noises are characterized only for narrow DC filter. Taking into account the given data, the gain in OSNR can be 10–12 dB.

Thus, when using in-line CD monitoring with a preliminary amplitude modulation of the RFCS, the gain relative to the OSNR compared to the monitoring

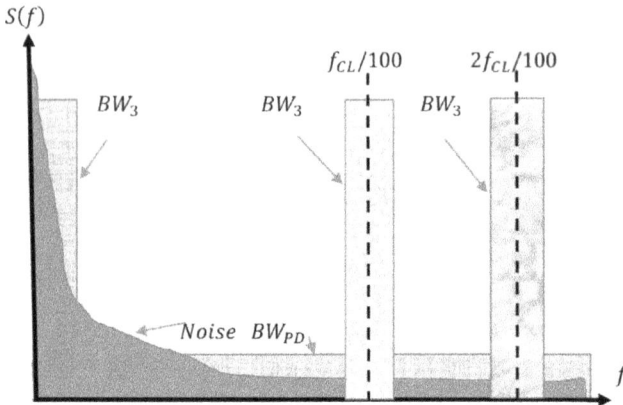

Figure 5.
Illustration for OSNR gain catch for three-frequency probing method: Noise—spectral characteristics of noise for photodetector realizations bandwidth BW_{PD}. Three-frequency probing method has complex gain parameters and characterizes only by one disadvantage of large current noise filtering on DC component.

at one frequency of the RFCS can be 10–13 dB. Thus, CD analysis on the RFCS can be carried out, starting with the classical OSNR in 3–5 dB.

4. Conclusion

We demonstrated a microwave photonic method for CD monitoring of a high-speed synchronization channel based on analyzing the reflectance spectrum of the built-in BNF with the preliminary amplitude modulation of the optical carrier and the RFCS method. The results of the simulation show that the proposed method of in-line monitoring makes it possible to determine the magnitude and direction of the filter shift by poly-harmonic probing. Thus, taking into account its position relative to the carrier, we will reduce the error in classical CD measuring which is usually equal to 10%/°C (1.5–3 dB). When using in-line CD monitoring with the preliminary amplitude modulation of the RFCS, the gain relative to OSNR compared to the monitoring at carrier frequency can be 10–13 dB. Thus, CD analysis by the RFSC method can be performed starting from the classical OSNR of 3–5 dB.

The application of such type monitoring methods for QKD-CMC system will allow us to suggest an even wider use in the transition to homodyne and heterodyne systems. It should be noted that their development is still carried out at a theoretical level and does not take into account the fact that with an increase in the length of telecommunication lines, the probability of increasing the influence of CD on the phase value of the coded components will increase significantly.

Acknowledgements

The Ministry of Science and Higher Education of the Russian Federation supported this work in frame of state R&D task to Kazan National Research Technical University n.a. A.N. Tupolev-KAI (base part, program "Asymmetry", task no. 8.6872.2017/8.9).

Author details

Oleg G. Morozov
Kazan National Research Technical University n.a. A.N. Tupolev-KAI,
Russian Federation, Russia

*Address all correspondence to: microoil@mail.ru

IntechOpen

References

[1] Merolla J-M, Mazurenko Y, Goedgebuer J-P, Duraffourg L, Porte H, Rhodes WT. Quantum cryptographic device using single-photon phase modulation. Physical Review. 1999;**A60** (3):1899-1905. DOI: 10.1103/ PhysRevA.60.1899

[2] Mérolla J-M, Mazurenko Y, Goedgebuer J-P, Porte H, Rhodes WT. Phase-modulation transmission system for quantum cryptography. Optics Letters. 1999;**24**:104-106. DOI: 10. 1364/OL.24.000104

[3] Duraffourg L, Merolla J-M, Goedgebuer J-P, Mazurenko Y, Rhodes WT. Compact transmission system using single-sideband modulation of light for quantum cryptography. Optics Letters. 2001;**26**(18):1427-1429. DOI: 10.1364/OL.26.001427

[4] Xavier GB, Weid JP. Modulation schemes for frequency coded quantum key distribution. Electronics Letters. 2005;**41**(10):607-608. DOI: 10.1049/el: 20050466

[5] Bloch M, McLaughlin SW, Merolla J-M, Patois F. Frequency-coded quantum key distribution. Optics Letters. 2007; **32**(3):301-303. DOI: 10.1364/ OL.32.000301

[6] Zang T, Yin Z-Q, Han Z-F, Guo G-C. A frequency-coded quantum key distribution scheme. Optics Communications. 2008;**281**:4800-4802. DOI: 10.1016/j.optcom.2008.06.009

[7] Kumar KP. Optical modulation schemes for frequency-coded quantum key distribution. In: Proceedings IEEE National Conference on Communications; 29-31 January 2010; Chennai, India. pp. 1-5. DOI: 10.1109/ NCC.2010.5430155

[8] Gleim AV, Egorov VI, Nazarov YV, Smirnov SV, Chistyakov VV, Bannik OI, et al. Secure polarization-independent subcarrier quantum key distribution in optical fiber channel using BB84 protocol with a strong reference. Optics Express. 2016;**24**(3):2619-2633. DOI: 10.1364/OE.24.002619

[9] Mora J, Ruiz-Alba A, Amaya W, Garcia-Muñoz V, Martinez A, Capmany J. Microwave photonic filtering scheme for BB84 subcarrier multiplexed quantum key distribution. In: Proceedings of IEEE Topical Meeting on Microwave Photonics. Montreal, QC, Canada; October 5-9, 2010; pp. 286-289. DOI: 10.1109/MWP. 2010.5664176

[10] Ruiz-Alba A, Calvo D, Garcia-Munoz V, Martinez A, Amaya W, Rozo JG, et al. Practical quantum key distribution based on BB84 protocol. Waves. 2011;1(**3**):4-14. Available from: https://riunet.upv.es/handle/10251/ 53967

[11] Morozov OG, Gabdulkhakov IM, Morozov GA, Zagrieva AR, Sarvarova LM. Frequency-coded quantum key distribution using amplitude-phase modulation. Proceedings of SPIE. 2015; **9807**:98071F. DOI: 10.1117/12.2230665

[12] Gabdulkhakov IM, Morozov OG, Morozov GA, Zastela MU, Tyajelova AA, Sarvarova LM. Frequency coding quantum key distribution channel based on serial photons amplitude modulation and phase commutation. Proceedings of SPIE. 2018;**10774**:107741Q. DOI: 10.1117/12.2322488

[13] Morozov OG, Sakhabutdinov AJ, Morozov GA, Gabdulkhakov IM. Universal microwave photonics approach to frequency-coded quantum key distribution. In: Advanced Technologies of Quantum Key Distribution. Sergiy Gnatyuk: IntechOpen; 2017. DOI: 10.5772/ intechopen.71974. Available from:

https://www.intechopen.com/books/ad
vanced-technologies-of-quantum-key-d
istribu-tion/universal-microwave-ph
otonics-approach-to-frequency-coded-
quantum-key-distribution

[14] Dubrovskaia VD, Chivilikhin SA.
Synchronization signal distortion in
subcarrier wave quantum key
distribution systems. Scientific and
Technical Journal of Information
Technologies, Mechanics and Optics.
2017;**17**(4):599-604. DOI: 10.17586/
2226-1494-2017-17-4-599-604

[15] Morozov OG, Il'in GI, Morozov GA,
Nureev II, Misbakhov RS. External
amplitude-phase modulation of laser
radiation for generation of microwave
frequency carriers and optical poly-
harmonic signals: An overview.
Proceedings of SPIE. 2015;**9807**:980711.
DOI: 10.1117/12.2231948

[16] Morozov OG, Aybatov DL.
Spectrum conversion investigation in
lithium niobate Mach-Zehnder
modulator. Proceedings of SPIE. 2010;
7523:75230D. DOI: 10.1117/12.854957

[17] Morozov OG. RZ, CS-RZ and soliton
generation for access networks
applications: Problems and variants of
decisions. Proceedings of SPIE. 2012;
8410:84100P. DOI: 10.1117/12. 923115

[18] Sadeev TS, Morozov OG.
Investigation and analysis of electro-
optical devices in implementation of
microwave photonic filters. Proceedings
of SPIE. 2012;**8410**:841007. DOI:
10.1117/12.923121

[19] Aybatov DL, Morozov OG, Sadeev
TS. Dual port MZM based optical comb
generator for all optical microwave
photonic devices. Proceedings of SPIE.
2011;**7992**:799202. DOI: 10.1117/
12.887273

[20] Il'In GI, Morozov OG, Il'In AG.
Theory of symmetrical two-frequency
signals and key aspects of its

application. Proceedings of SPIE. 2014;
9156:91560M. DOI: 10.1117/12.2054753

[21] Morozov GA, Morozov GA, Il'in GI,
Il'in AG. Instantaneous frequency
measurements of microwave signal with
serial amplitude-phase modulation
conversion of optical carrier.
Proceedings of SPIE. 2014;**9533**:95330Q.
DOI: 10.1117/12.2181435

[22] Morozov OG, Talipov AA,
Nurgazizov MR, Denisenko PE, Vasilets
AA. Instantaneous frequency
measurement of microwave signals in
optical range using "frequency-
amplitude" conversion in the π-phase
shifted fibre Bragg grating. Proceedings
of SPIE. 2014;**9136**:91361B. DOI:
10.1117/12.2051126

[23] Gasulla I, Capmany J. Analytical
model and figures of merit for filtered
microwave photonic links.
Optics Express. 2011;**19**(20):
19758-19774. DOI: 10.1364/
OE.19.019758

[24] Capmany J, Fernandez-Pousa CR.
Quantum modelling of electro-optic
modulators. Laser and Photonics
Reviews. 2011;**5**(6):750-772. DOI:
10.1002/lpor.201000038

[25] Yang J, Yu C, Yang Y, et al.
PMD-Insensitive CD monitoring based
on rf clock power ratio measurement
with optical notch filter. IEEE Photonics
Technology Letters. 2011;**23**(21):1576-
1578. DOI: 10.1109/LPT.2011.2164519

[26] Andreev VD, Kazarov VU, Morozov
OG, Nureev II, et al. CD monitoring
based on Bragg Notch filter reflection
spectrum analysis. In: Proceedings 2018
Systems of Signal Synchronization,
Generating and Processing in
Telecommunications Conference
(SYNCHROINFO). 2018. pp. 1-4. DOI:
10.1109/SYNCHROINFO.2018.8456927

[27] Morozov OG, Il'in GI, Morozov GA,
Sadeev TS. Synthesis of two-frequency

symmetrical radiation and its application in fiber optical structures monitoring. In: Yasin M, Harun SW, Arof H, editors. Fiber Optic Sensors. Rijeka, Croatia: IntechOpen; 2012. DOI: 10.5772/27304. Available from: https://www.intechopen.com/books/fiber-optic-sensors/synthesis-of-two-frequency-symmetrical-radiation-and-its-application-in-fiber-optical-structures-mon

[28] Sakhbiev TR, Morozov OG, Sakhabutdinov AJ, Faskhutdinov LM, Nureev II. Optical vector network analyzer based on unbalanced amplitude-phase modulation. In: Proceedings of 2018 Systems of Signal Synchronization, Generating and Processing in Telecommunications (SYNCHROINFO) Conference. 2018. pp. 1-4. DOI: 10.1109/SYNCHROINFO.2018.8456939

[29] Morozov OG, Morozov GA, Nureev II, et al. Optical vector network analyzer based on amplitude-phase modulation. Proceedings of SPIE. 2016;**9807**:980717. DOI: 10.1117/12.2232993

[30] Morozov OG, Denisenko PE, Denisenko EP, et al. Fiber-optic Bragg sensors with special spectrum shapes for climatic test systems. Proceedings of SPIE. 2017;**10342**:1034217. DOI: 10.1117/12.2270750

[31] Pan Z, Yu C, Willner AE. Optical performance monitoring for the next generation optical communication networks. Optical Fiber Technology. 2010;**16**:20-45. DOI: 10.1016/j.yofte.2009.09.007

Chapter 2

Quantum Key Distribution (QKD) over Software-Defined Optical Networks

Yongli Zhao, Yuan Cao, Xiaosong Yu and Jie Zhang

Abstract

Optical network security is attracting increasing research interest. Currently, software-defined optical network (SDON) has been proposed to increase network intelligence (e.g., flexibility and programmability) which is gradually moving toward industrialization. However, a variety of new threats are emerging in SDONs. Data encryption is an effective way to secure communications in SDONs. However, classical key distribution methods based on the mathematical complexity will suffer from increasing computational power and attack algorithms in the near future. Noticeably, quantum key distribution (QKD) is now being considered as a secure mechanism to provision information-theoretically secure secret keys for data encryption, which is a potential technique to protect communications from security attacks in SDONs. This chapter introduces the basic principles and enabling technologies of QKD. Based on the QKD enabling technologies, an architecture of QKD over SDONs is presented. Resource allocation problem is elaborated in detail and is classified into wavelength allocation, time-slot allocation, and secret key allocation problems in QKD over SDONs. Some open issues and challenges such as survivability, cost optimization, and key on demand (KoD) for QKD over SDONs are discussed.

Keywords: optical network, SDON, security, QKD, architecture, resource allocation

1. Introduction

As more than two billion kilometers of optical fibers deployed worldwide [1], optical networks have currently served as one of the most important underlying infrastructures. Large confidential data transferred daily over the Internet relies on the secrecy and reliability of data channels (DChs) in optical networks against several types of cyberattacks, e.g., physically tapping or listening to the residual crosstalk from an adjacent channel [2, 3]. With the evolution of network intelligence, software-defined networking (SDN) [4] is emerging and developing toward practical application, which is a promising technique to add flexibility and programmability in the optical layer. Hence, software-defined optical networking (SDON) is potential to become the next generation optical network architecture [5]. However, the control and configuration signaling messages transferred via the control channels (CChs) are also facing a variety of security attacks, e.g., anomaly attacks and intrusion attacks [6]. Therefore, two essential channels (i.e., DChs transferring sensitive data/services and CChs interchanging control/configuration messages) are vulnerable to cyberattacks in SDONs.

Data encryption is an effective way to enhance the security of SDONs. However, classical key distribution methods are based on the mathematical and computational complexities, which will suffer from increased computational power and developed quantum computing in the near future [7]. Quantum key distribution (QKD) is a promising technique to secure key exchange and protect communications from security attacks in SDONs [8]. It can achieve information-theoretic security based on the fundamentals of quantum physics, such as the Heisenberg uncertainty principle and quantum no-cloning theorem [9, 10]. Moreover, these fundamentals guarantee that the senders or receivers can detect the presence of any third party who is trying to obtain the secret keys. Optical fibers can be used in QKD systems to achieve good transmission performance of quantum signals. Nevertheless, the dark fibers utilized for QKD systems are inconvenient and expensive, while a potential solution is to use wavelength division multiplexing (WDM) technique for QKD integration in existing optical networks [11]. A lot of experiments and field trials have demonstrated the feasibility and practicability of integrating QKD into optical networks [12–18]. Therefore, based on above works, the objective of this chapter is to find how to deploy and employ QKD to enhance the security of SDONs.

2. Basic principles and enabling technologies of QKD

2.1 Principle of point-to-point QKD

The basic principle of point-to-point QKD is introduced based on the first invented QKD protocol, i.e., BB84 protocol proposed by Bennett and Brassard in 1984 [19], as illustrated in **Figure 1**. Nowadays, BB84 protocol is widely used in practical QKD systems [20, 21]. The BB84 protocol based QKD process is summarized in the following three stages.

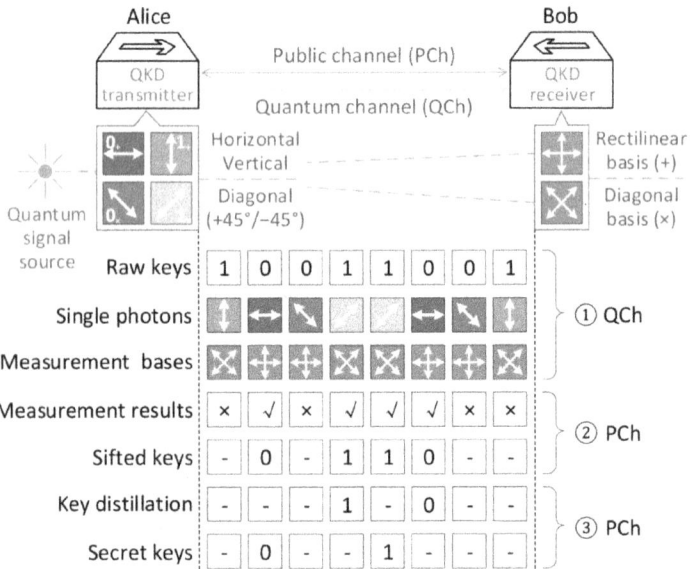

Figure 1.
Principle of point-to-point QKD based on BB84 protocol.

1. Qubit exchange: QKD transmitter (called Alice) generates qubits and sends them to the QKD receiver (called Bob) via a quantum channel (QCh). The qubits are generated by encoding a string of classical bits into single-polarization photons with different states. For instance, the horizontal, vertical, and diagonal ±45° polarization states randomly selected from two conjugate bases (i.e., rectilinear$_+$ and diagonal$_x$) are encoded with 0_+, 1_+, 1_x, and 0_x, respectively. In order to achieve accurate qubit synchronization, a clock channel is also required here. Bob receives the incoming qubits and measures each single-polarization photon with one of the two conjugate bases (i.e., rectilinear$_+$ and diagonal$_x$), and it will record the measurement results and the selected bases.

2. Key sifting: Alice and Bob exchange their selected bases via a pubic channel (PCh), and then discard the qubits sent and measured with different conjugate bases. The remaining qubits will be decoded into a string of classical bits as sifted keys.

3. Key distillation: For error estimation and correction, a random substring of classical bits in sifted keys is exchanged and compared between Alice and Bob via the PCh. Finally, privacy amplification and authentication are implemented to decide the remaining secure bits as secret keys.

Additionally, to improve the secret key rate in QKD systems in practice, decoy-state can be integrated with BB84 protocol to basically reach the single-photon sources performance and estimate the number of single-polarization photons detected by Bob more precisely [8].

2.2 Trusted repeaters for distance extension

The secret key rate and distance of QKD are limited due to the attenuation of weak quantum signals in QChs. This limitation can be overcome by using quantum repeaters, but they are beyond any practical technologies today [22]. A compromise and a practical solution to this challenge are using trusted repeaters, and this technique has been applied in the deployment of most QKD networks up to date [23–25]. In a QKD network based on trusted repeaters, the secret keys generated on the first QKD link can be relayed to the destination node by encrypting them with the secret keys generated in the intermediate nodes. One-time pad algorithm is applied for encryption to ensure the information-theoretic security of secret keys verified by Shannon [26], while the size of secret keys generated and encrypted here should be the same. Hence, secret keys are known by all intermediate nodes, making the secret key secure only as long as all the repeaters are trusted.

An example of QKD distance extension based on a trusted repeater between the source and destination nodes is illustrated in **Figure 2**. The QKD transmitter in the source node establishes a QKD link with the forthcoming QKD receiver in the intermediate node, whereas the QKD receiver in the destination node establishes a QKD link with the previous QKD transmitter in the intermediate node. Both QKD links produce, independently, secret keys Sk_1 and Sk_2 with the same key size. Then, the secret key Sk_1 is encrypted with the secret key Sk_2 and relayed to the destination node. Specifically, secret key Sk_1 can be used later to secure communications between the source and destination nodes. This relay process can continue with any amount of intermediate nodes, but each intermediate node with the trusted repeater will know the secret key information.

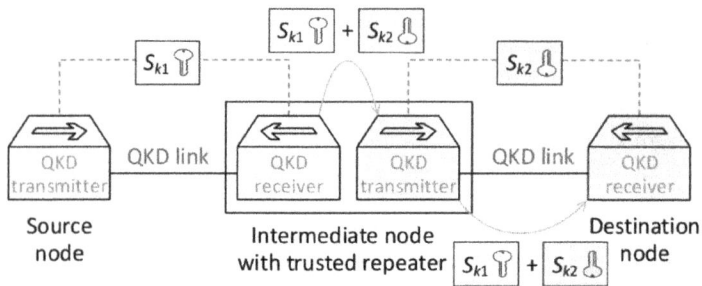

Figure 2.
An example of QKD distance extension based on a trusted repeater between the source and destination nodes.

Figure 3.
An example of QKP for secret key provisioning between Node-A and Node-B.

2.3 Quantum key pool (QKP) for secret key provisioning

Currently, the secret key rate in most QKD systems can only reach 1–2 Mbit/s over a 50 km fiber link [27]. Therefore, the efficient management of precious secret key resources is important. Recently, quantum key pool (QKP) technique is proposed in QKD networks to timely provision secret keys for satisfying the security demands of communications crossing the networks [6], which is beneficial to enhance secret key management when the QKD develops from point-to-point links to networks. The secret keys generated between the two end nodes can be stored in the key store (KS) which is embedded in each of the two end-nodes and can be managed by a QKP. QKP will know the real-time remaining number of secret keys in the KS, which can decide when to connect the QKD link for secret key provisioning. Hence, efficient QKP construction is beneficial for efficiently employing QKD.

An example of QKP between Node-A and Node-B is illustrated in **Figure 3**. The QKD node is composed of several components based on the existing QKD technologies, e.g., QKD transceiver, trusted repeater, and switch [23]. The generated secret keys between QKD Node-A and QKD Node-B can be stored in KS-A and KS-B, which are embedded in Node-A and Node-B, respectively. Specifically, the generated secret keys are managed by QKP_{A-B} to monitor the real-time remaining number of secret keys and provision secret keys between Node-A and Node-B.

3. QKD over SDON Architecture

An architecture of QKD over SDONs is illustrated in **Figure 4(a)**, which consists of four layers from top to bottom: application (App) layer, control layer, QKD layer,

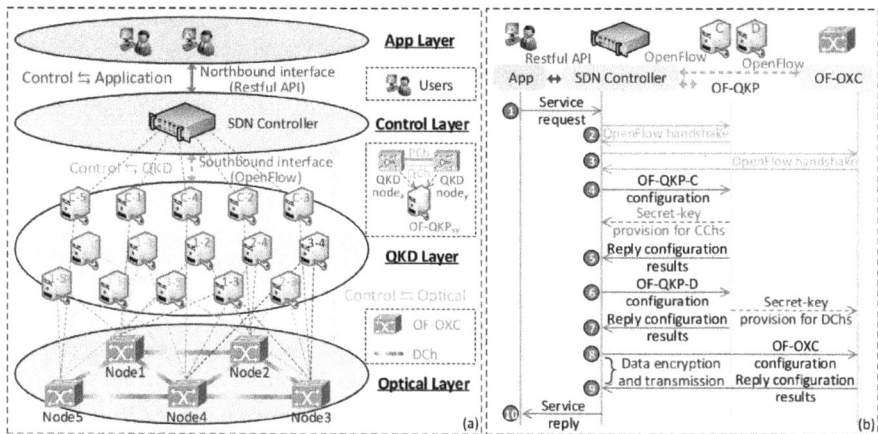

Figure 4.
(a) QKD over SDON architecture; and (b) the configuration signaling procedure.

and optical layer. This architecture is different from the previous QKD-integrated optical networks [11] and decouples QKD layer from the optical layer via constructing several QKPs in the QKD layer. Two types of QKPs are constructed to enhance the security of control signaling messages over the CChs, and confidential data services over the DChs, respectively. The QKP between the SDN controller and each node is called QKP-C (i.e., QKP-CCh), whereas the QKP between two nodes is called QKP-D (i.e., QKP-DCh). The SDN controller in the control layer controls and manages the QKD layer and optical layer via the southbound interface protocol (e.g., OpenFlow and NETCONF). Here we use OpenFlow protocol as an example. The SDN controller is capable of realizing flexible and programmable global optical network management, which can be utilized as the effective implementation technique for control layer. Moreover, it has been demonstrated in the recent study on time-shared QKD resources in SDN-controlled optical networks [28].

Optical layer and QKD layer can share the fiber bandwidth resources from existing WDM networks, in which at least two wavelengths need to be utilized as QCh and PCh to construct OpenFlow-enabled QKPs (OF-QKPs), and then the remaining wavelength resources can be utilized to transport confidential data services. The constructed OF-QKPs can provision secret keys to guarantee the security of CChs and DChs. In addition, OpenFlow-enabled optical cross connects (OF-OXCs) are placed in the optical layer. The SDN controller is capable of managing the entire network efficiently, whereas the OF-QKPs and OF-OXCs are capable of operating based on the instructions from SDN controller.

The App layer generates service requests with different security demands and interacts with control layer via the Restful API, in which Restful API is applied as northbound interface protocol. Based on the different security demands, CChs and DChs may require different number of secret keys. In particular, this QKD over SDON architecture can manage and control the network-wide secret key resources, which is beneficial to adapt diverse security demands and dynamic scenarios.

Figure 4(b) illustrates the configuration signaling procedure among the four layers in QKD over SDON architecture. This procedure can be described in the following five stages: (1) upon receiving a service request (e.g., the service request from Node 1 to Node 2) from the App, SDN controller first computes/selects path and then implements OpenFlow handshake with related OF-OXCs as well as OF-QKPs on the selected path; (2) after the establishment of first stage, OF-QKP-C$_1$ and OF-QKP-C$_2$ are configured by the SDN controller to provision secret keys for control/configuration messages over the CChs; (3) OF-QKP-D$_{1-2}$ is configured by the SDN controller to provision secret keys for the service request from OF-OXC$_1$ to OF-OXC$_2$ over the DCh; (4) the SDN controller configures OF-OXC$_1$ and OF-OXC$_2$ to encrypt data and transport the service; and (5) at last, SDN controller replies to the App.

4. Resource allocation in QKD over SDONs

4.1 Wavelength allocation

Since three types of channels (i.e., QChs, PChs, and DChs) are coexisting in a single fiber with WDM technique, wavelength allocation for these three types of channels becomes an essential issue. The total number of wavelengths for QChs, PChs, and DChs should conform to existing WDM networks, e.g., 40 wavelengths (with 100 GHz channel spacing) or 80 wavelengths (with 50 GHz channel spacing). Given the DCh is usually located at C-band (1530–1565 nm) in existing WDM networks, some previous studies have demonstrated QKD at O-band (1260–1360 nm) [29, 30] to achieve strong isolation from data transmission. Nevertheless, the faint quantum signals may suffer from more losses at O-band compared with C-band, which will limit the transmission distance and rate. Therefore, the three types of channels can be placed at C-band to achieve better quantum-signal transmission performance, as illustrated in **Figure 5**.

In particular, the physical layer impairments (e.g., Raman scattering and four-wave-mixing effects) induced by PCh and DCh may have negative impacts on the QCh transmission performance. Raman scattering effects can be effectively reduced by placing the QCh at high frequency [31], thereby the wavelength reserved as QCh starts from 1530 nm. Besides, four-wave-mixing effects can be reduced by allocating 200 GHz guard band between QCh and other classical channels (i.e., PChs and DChs) [17]. Moreover, appropriate channel isolation and stable QKD operation can be achieved by using multistage band-stop filtering technique [32]. The PCh that transmits classical signals for key sifting and distillation as introduced in the principle of point-to-point QKD can share the same wavelengths with DCh or utilize the dedicated wavelengths at fiber C-band. The latter can be selected to ensure one-to-one relationship between the PCh and QCh, although the wavelength resources for data transmission may be degraded. This is because allocating dedicated wavelengths for QCh and PCh is essential in a stable scenario. The intermediate nodes with trusted repeaters and erbium-doped fiber amplifiers (EDFAs) can be deployed for QCh and PCh/DCh, respectively, to extend quantum and classical signal transmission distance, in which EDFA bypass scheme [30, 33] can be utilized

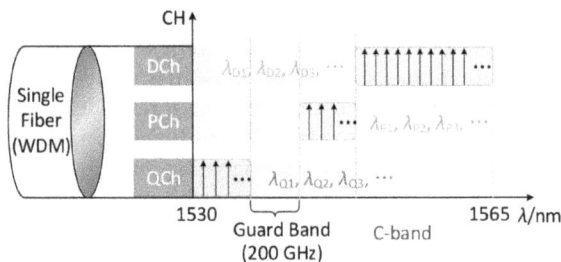

Figure 5.
Wavelength allocation for the three types of channels (i.e., QChs, PChs, and DChs) over the C-band in a single fiber.

for quantum and classical signal coexistence in a single fiber to suppress the noise from the EDFA's amplified spontaneous emission (ASE).

4.2 Time-slot allocation

Given the finite wavelength resources in a single fiber and the high cost of establishing QChs and PChs, each wavelength for QCh/PCh is segmented into multiple time slots according to optical time division multiplexing (OTDM) technique [34]. Hence, each time slot can be utilized to establish a QCh/PCh for improving resource utilization. We assume that the secret keys provisioned for a service request with specific security demand are exchanged between the source and destination nodes within a fixed time t, thereby each QCh/PCh occupies a time slot. On the basis of the principle of point-to-point QKD described above, t consists of channel estimation and calibration time, qubit exchange time, key sifting time, and key distillation time. In particular, the scattering and loss may impact the secret key rate between two nodes, which will lead to different number of secret keys shared between different node pairs within t in QKD over SDONs. In the network model, to fix t with a realistic and simplified manner, the size of t can be set as the secret key exchange time for a fixed key size (e.g., 128, 192, and 256 bit while using AES encryption algorithm [35]) under the worst scenario in QKD over SDONs.

Additionally, to prevent attacks for enhancing the data encryption security, the secret keys provisioned for each service request with specific security demand can be updated in a period T. The parameter, T, is the period after which the secret key must be changed between two nodes. The security level increases while decreasing the value of T. This is because the secret keys provisioned for a service request with specific security demand are updated more frequently, thereby increasing the difficulty of cracking the encryption key by a third party [36]. Accordingly, considering the key-updating period, time-slot allocation for QCh/PCh becomes a new topic to be studied. Also, routing, wavelength, and time-slot allocation (RWTA) strategy for establishing the three types of channels (i.e., QChs, PChs, and DChs) needs to be considered.

For instance, **Figure 6** illustrates two security level configuration solutions, in which the parameter, t, is the secret key exchange time between the source and destination nodes for each service request with specific security demand, and the parameter, T, is the key-updating period ($t < T$, which guarantees that the secret keys can be exchanged within a period). In solution 1, we fix T for all the QCh/PCh wavelengths and each service request with specific security demand has the same security level value of T. Note that the QCh/PCh wavelengths are the wavelengths in WDM optical networks that are reserved as QCh/PCh. The solution 1 can only provide one security level, which may limit the flexibility of security demands of service requests. However, service requests triggered from numerous security-hungry applications may have different security demands with different security levels. Hence, each QCh wavelength has a flexible T values in solution 2, thereby different security levels can be provisioned. For different service requests with security demands, this solution can provision more security level types.

4.3 Secret key allocation

Data encryption algorithms need to be considered for CChs and DChs while performing secret key allocation. One-time pad (OTP) encryption algorithm was invented to achieve information-theoretic security, in which the secret key size should be as long as the data size [26]. Hence, OTP encryption algorithm requires much execution time/storage to perform data encryption, which is difficult to be

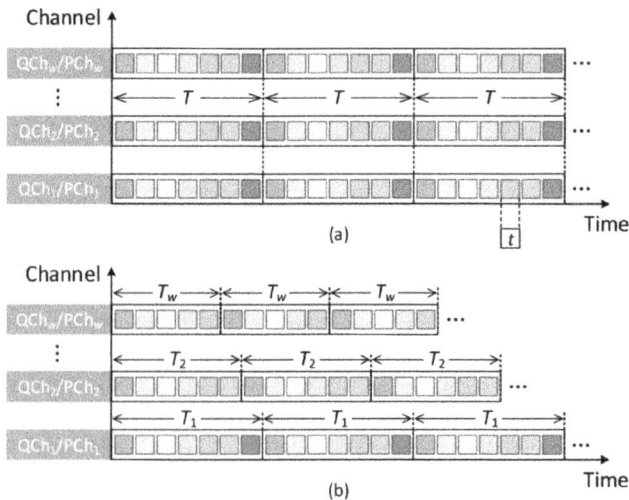

Figure 6.
Two security-level provisioning solutions: (a) solution 1: fixed T for all the QCh/PCh wavelengths; and (b) solution 2: flexible T for each QCh/PCh wavelength.

utilized for high-bit-rate data encryption in SDONs and has negative impacts on the efficiency of SDONs. Nevertheless, symmetric encryption algorithms [37] can be used to perform large amount of data encryption with small secret key size and fast execution time. A commonly used symmetric encryption algorithm is advanced encryption standard (AES) algorithm, which can be integrated with QKD to implement high-bit-rate data encryption [38, 39]. Using secret key lengths of 128, 192, and 256 bit, the AES algorithm can encrypt/decrypt large amount of data in blocks of 128 bit [35]. Hence, the secret key receiving module and data encryption module can be added in optical transport nodes to perform secret key communication and processing.

Nevertheless, the third party can eavesdrop a sequence of encrypted data to crack the secret keys while using AES algorithm. Then, two important factors, i.e., data size and data transmission time, need to be considered during a crack [40, 41]. In order to degrade the probability of encrypted data being cracked, the secret key can be frequently changed between two nodes based on the key-updating period. Key updating is essential to enhance the security of data encryption while using AES algorithm to secure CChs and DChs. Accordingly, the time complexity and data complexity of attacks can be considered for key updating in which time complexity is the maximum available time for a secret key and data complexity is the maximum encrypted data size by a secret key. The security level increases with the increase of secret key length or the decrease of secret key-updating period. Therefore, we can qualitatively evaluate the security level based on secret key length and updating period.

Given the secret key resources are limited and precious in QKPs, the secret key allocation issue for CChs and DChs needs to be solved. The control/configuration messages transmitted over the CChs in SDONs are usually at megabit-per-second transmission rate, which are low compared with the data complexity of attacks [40]. Accordingly, secret key allocation and updating are accomplished for each CCh in the SDON to enhance its security. Through the path of a data service, each node along the path will be configured by the SDN controller via the corresponding CCh. According to the specific security demand of each CCh, QKP-C allocates the required secret keys between SDN controller and each node to enhance the security

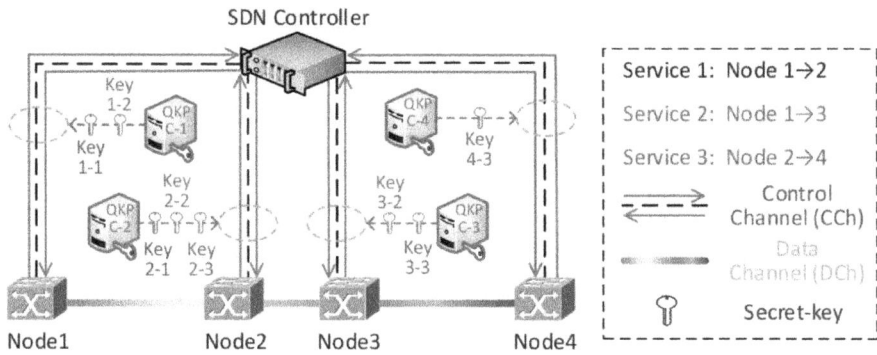

Figure 7.
Secret key allocation and updating for CChs.

of each CCh. Hence, we can allocate different number of secret keys to CChs between SDN controller and each node for encrypting/decrypting the control/configuration messages. As illustrated with an example in **Figure 7**, Keyx_y denotes the required number of secret keys in which x and y represent the node serial number and service serial number, respectively. Key$_{1-1}$/Key$_{2-1}$ is allocated to CChs between the SDN controller and Node 1/Node 2 for Service 1, whereas Key$_{1-2}$/Key$_{2-2}$/Key$_{3-2}$ is allocated to CChs between the SDN controller and Node 1/Node 2/Node 3 for Service 2.

The required number of secret keys for each data service over the DChs is associated with the secret key length and updating period. The QKP-D can allocate the required number of secret keys to enhance the security of data services over the DChs in SDONs. As illustrated with an example in **Figure 8**, three data services (i.e., r_1, r_2, and r_3) have different security demands. In **Figure 8(a)** and **(b)**, we consider the time complexity of attacks (i.e., T_y) and data complexity (i.e., D_y) of attacks for secret key updating, respectively, in which the parameter, y, represents the data service serial number. Based on AES algorithm, the required secret key lengths of r_1, r_2, and r_3 are 128, 192, and 256 bit, respectively. Additionally, as shown in **Figure 8(a)**, the required secret key-updating periods of r_1, r_2, and r_3 are T_1, T_2, and T_3 ($T_1 < T_2 < T_3$), respectively; whereas in **Figure 8(b)**, the required secret key-updating periods of r_1, r_2, and r_3 are D_1, D_2, and D_3 ($D_1 < D_2 < D_3$), respectively. Specifically, the data service with longer secret key length and shorter secret key-updating period demands shows higher security level and will require more secret keys to be allocated for data encryption. Thus, routing, wavelength, and secret key allocation (RWKA) strategy for CChs and DChs in a timely manner on demand is necessary to be considered.

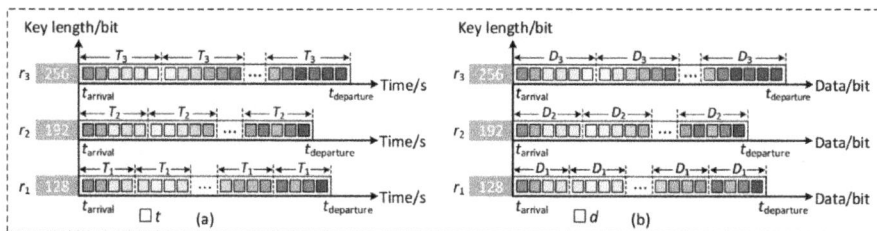

Figure 8.
Secret key allocation and updating for services with different security requirements based on (a) case 1: time complexity of attacks and (b) case 2: data complexity of attacks.

5. Open issues and challenges

5.1 Survivability for QKD over SDONs

QKD can provide secret keys for end-to-end paths and improve the security of SDONs. However, how to guarantee survivability in a QKD over SDON is an important topic. QCh and PCh should be protected simultaneously in a QKD over SDON. Especially due to the utilization of key-updating period (security level) with different time slots, protection action will occur at a subwavelength level. Synchronization might also be a difficult problem for QCh, PCh, and DCh.

5.2 Cost optimization for QKD over SDONs

In a QKD network, two types of nodes should be deployed, i.e., QKD node and intermediate node with trusted repeaters. Also, several wavelength channels in existing WDM optical networks should be planned as QChs and PChs. In practice, different number of nodes and QChs/PChs may produce different costs and performance for QKD over SDONs. Accordingly, how to optimize the cost of deploying QKD over SDONs while satisfying the performance requirements is another open issue.

5.3 Key on demand (KoD) for QKD over SDONs

The secret key rate (i.e., the generation of secret keys in bits per second) in current advanced QKD systems is extremely low compared with the gigabit data transmission over each wavelength in WDM optical networks. Increasing the number of nodes and QChs/PChs can further increase the secret key rate, but it will also drastically increase the system complexity and power consumption. Thus, the use of an efficient key on demand (KoD) scheme to achieve efficient secret key resource usage while satisfying security requirements of CChs and DChs is also essential for QKD over SDONs.

6. Conclusions

This chapter provides a brief introduction to the basic principles and enabling technologies of QKD. Based on the QKD-enabling technologies, an architecture of QKD over SDONs is presented. Resource allocation problem is elaborated in detail and is classified into wavelength allocation, time-slot allocation, and secret key allocation problems in QKD over SDONs. Finally, several open issues and challenges are discussed.

Author details

Yongli Zhao*, Yuan Cao, Xiaosong Yu and Jie Zhang
State Key Laboratory of Information Photonics and Optical Communications,
Beijing University of Posts and Telecommunications, Beijing, China

*Address all correspondence to: yonglizhao@bupt.edu.cn

IntechOpen

References

[1] Winzer PJ. Scaling optical fiber networks: Challenges and solutions. Optics & Photonics News. 2015;**26**(3):28-35. DOI: 10.1364/OPN.26.3.000028

[2] Fok MP, Wang Z, Deng Y, Prucnal PR. Optical layer security in fiber-optic networks. IEEE Transactions on Information Forensics and Security. 2011;**6**(3):725-736. DOI: 10.1109/TIFS.2011.2141990

[3] Skorin-Kapov N, Furdek M, Zsigmond S, Wosinska L. Physical-layer security in evolving optical networks. IEEE Communications Magazine. 2016;**54**(8):110-117. DOI: 10.1109/MCOM.2016.7537185

[4] Rawat DB, Reddy SR. Software defined networking architecture, security and energy efficiency: A survey. IEEE Communication Surveys and Tutorials. 2017; **19**(1):325-346. DOI: 10.1109/COMST.2016.2618874

[5] Zhao Y, He R, Chen H, Zhang J, Ji Y, et al. Experimental performance evaluation of software defined networking (SDN) based data communication networks for large scale flexi-grid optical networks. Optics Express. 2014;**22**(8):9538-9547. DOI: 10.1364/OE.22.009538

[6] Cao Y, Zhao Y, Colman-Meixner C, Yu X, Zhang J. Key on demand (KoD) for software-defined optical networks secured by quantum key distribution (QKD). Optics Express. 2017;**25**(22):26453-26467. DOI: 10.1364/OE.25.026453

[7] Schreiber LR, Bluhm H. Toward a silicon-based quantum computer. Science. 2018;**359**(6374):393-394. DOI: 10.1126/science.aar6209

[8] Lo HK, Curty M, Tamaki K. Secure quantum key distribution. Nature Photonics. 2014;**8**:595-604. DOI: 10.1038/nphoton.2014.149

[9] Maeda W, Tanaka A, Takahashi S, Tajima A, Tomita A. Technologies for quantum key distribution networks integrated with optical communication networks. IEEE Journal of Selected Topics in Quantum Electronics. 2009;**15**(6):1591-1601. DOI: 10.1109/JSTQE.2009.2032664

[10] Lo HK, Chau HF. Unconditional security of quantum key distribution over arbitrarily long distances. Science. 1999;**283**:2050-2056. DOI: 10.1126/science.283.5410.2050

[11] Cao Y, Zhao Y, Yu X, Wu Y. Resource assignment strategy in optical networks integrated with quantum key distribution. Journal of Optical Communications and Networking. 2017;**9**(11):995-1004. DOI: 10.1364/JOCN.9.000995

[12] Mao Y, Wang B-X, Zhao C, Wang G, Wang R, et al. Integrating quantum key distribution with classical communications in backbone fiber network. Optics Express. 2018;**26**(5):6010-6020. DOI: 10.1364/OE.26.006010

[13] Karinou F, Brunner HH, Fung C-HF, Comandar LC, Bettelli S, et al. Toward the integration of CV quantum key distribution in deployed optical networks. IEEE Photonics Technology Letters. 2018;**30**(7):650-653. DOI: 10.1109/LPT.2018.2810334

[14] Patel KA, Dynes JF, Lucamarini M, Choi I, Sharpe AW, et al. Quantum key distribution for 10 Gb/s dense wavelength division multiplexing networks. Applied Physics Letters. 2014;**104**(5):051123. DOI: 10.1063/1.4864398

[15] Zhao Y, Cao Y, Wang W, Wang H, Yu X, et al. Resource allocation in

optical networks secured by quantum key distribution. IEEE Communications Magazine. 2018;**56**(8):130-137. DOI: 10.1109/MCOM.2018.1700656

[16] Cao Y, Zhao Y, Wu Y, Yu X, Zhang J. Time-scheduled quantum key distribution (QKD) over WDM networks. Journal of Lightwave Technology. 2018;**36**(16):3382-3395. DOI: 10.1109/JLT.2018.2834949

[17] Peters NA, Toliver P, Chapuran TE, Runser RJ, McNown SR, et al. Dense wavelength multiplexing of 1550 nm QKD with strong classical channels in reconfigurable networking environments. New Journal of Physics. 2009;**11**(4):045012. DOI: 10.1088/1367-2630/11/4/045012

[18] Qi B, Zhu W, Qian L, Lo HK. Feasibility of quantum key distribution through a dense wavelength division multiplexing network. New Journal of Physics. 2010;**12**(10):103042. DOI: 10.1088/1367-2630/12/10/103042

[19] Bennett CH, Brassard G. Quantum cryptography: Public key distribution and coin tossing. In: Proceedings of IEEE International Conference on Computers, Systems, and Signal Processing; Bangalore, India; 1984

[20] QuantumCTek [Internet]. Available from: http://www.quantum-info.com/English/

[21] Toshiba QKD system [Internet]. Available from: https://www.toshiba.eu/eu/Cambridge-Research-Laboratory/Quantum-Information/Quantum-Key-Distribution/Toshiba-QKD-system/

[22] Elkouss D, Martinez-Mateo J, Ciurana A, Martin V. Secure optical networks based on quantum key distribution and weakly trusted repeaters. Journal of Optical Communications and Networking. 2013;**5**(4):316-328. DOI: 10.1364/JOCN.5.000316

[23] Peev M, Pacher C, Alléaume R, Barreiro C, Bouda J, et al. The SECOQC quantum key distribution network in Vienna. New Journal of Physics. 2009;**11**(7):075001. DOI: 10.1088/1367-2630/11/7/075001

[24] Sasaki M, Fujiwara M, Ishizuka H, Klaus W, Wakui K, et al. Field test of quantum key distribution in the Tokyo QKD network. Optics Express. 2011;**19**(11):10387-10409. DOI: 10.1364/OE.19.010387

[25] Wang S, Chen W, Yin Z-Q, Li H-W, He D-Y, et al. Field and long-term demonstration of a wide area quantum key distribution network. Optics Express. 2014;**22**(18):21739-21756. DOI: 10.1364/OE.22.021739

[26] Shannon CE. Communication theory of secrecy systems. Bell Labs Technical Journal. 1949;**28**(4):656-715

[27] Gleim AV, Egorov VI, Nazarov YV, Smirnov SV, Chistyakov VV, et al. Secure polarization-independent subcarrier quantum key distribution in optical fiber channel using BB84 protocol with a strong reference. Optics Express. 2016;**24**(3):2619-2633. DOI: 10.1364/OE.24.002619

[28] Aguado A, Hugues-Salas E, Haigh PA, Marhuenda J, Price AB, et al. Secure NFV orchestration over an SDN-controlled optical network with time-shared quantum key distribution resources. Journal of Lightwave Technology. 2017;**35**(8):1357-1362. DOI: 10.1109/JLT.2016.2646921

[29] Runser RJ, Chapuran TE, Toliver P, Goodman MS, Jackel J, et al. Demonstration of 1.3 μm quantum key distribution (QKD) compatibility with 1.5 μm metropolitan wavelength division multiplexed (WDM) systems." In: Proceedings of OFC/NFOEC; March 2005; Anaheim, California, United States. DOI: 10.1109/OFC.2005.192752. p. OWI2

[30] Nweke NI, Runser RJ, McNown SR, Khurgin JB, Chapuran TE, et al. EDFA bypass and filtering architecture enabling QKD+WDM coexistence on mid-span amplified links. In: Proceedings of CLEO/QELS; May 2006; Long Beach, California, United States. DOI: 10.1109/CLEO.2006.4628431. p. CWQ7

[31] Kawahara H, Medhipour A, Inoue K. Effect of spontaneous Raman scattering on quantum channel wavelength-multiplexed with classical channel. Optics Communications. 2011;**284**:691-696. DOI: 10.1016/j.optcom.2010.09.051

[32] Wang LJ, Chen LK, Ju L, Xu ML, Zhao Y, et al. Experimental multiplexing of quantum key distribution with classical optical communication. Applied Physics Letters. 2015;**106**(8):081108. DOI: 10.1063/1.4913483

[33] Aleksic S, Winkler D, Hipp F, Poppe A, Franzl G, Schrenk B. Towards a smooth integration of quantum key distribution in metro networks. In: Proceedings of ICTON; July 2014; Graz, Austria. DOI: 10.1109/ICTON.2014.6876369

[34] Wen B, Sivalingam KM. Routing, wavelength and time-slot assignment in time division multiplexed wavelength-routed optical WDM networks. In: Proceedings of INFOCOM; June 2002; New York, USA. pp. 1442-1450. DOI: 10.1109/INFCOM.2002.1019395

[35] National Institute of Standards and Technology (NIST). Advanced Encryption Standard (AES). Federal Information Processing Standard (FIPS) 197. Nov. 2001

[36] Taha M, Schaumont P. Key-updating for leakage resiliency with application to AES modes of operation. IEEE Transactions on Information Forensics and Security. 2015;**10**(3):519-528. DOI: 10.1109/TIFS.2014.2383359

[37] Jouguet P, Kunz-Jacques S, Debuisschert T, Fossier S, Diamanti E, et al. Field test of classical symmetric encryption with continuous variables quantum key distribution. Optics Express. 2012;**20**(13):14030-14041. DOI: 10.1364/OE.20.014030

[38] Eraerds P, Walenta N, Legr'e M, Gisin N, Zbinden H. Quantum key distribution and 1 Gbit/s data encryption over a single fibre. New Journal of Physics. 2010;**12**(6):063027. DOI: 10.1088/1367-2630/12/6/063027

[39] Sharma G, Kalra S. A novel scheme for data security in cloud computing using quantum cryptography. In: Proceedings of AICTC 2016; August 2016; Bikaner, India. DOI: 10.1145/2979779.2979816

[40] Assche GV. Quantum Cryptography and Secret-Key Distillation. Cambridge University; 2006

[41] Derbez P, Fouque PA, Jean J. Improved key recovery attacks on reduced-round AES in the single-key setting. In: Proceedings of EUROCRYPT 2013; May 2013; Athens, Greece. DOI: 10.1007/978-3-642-38348-9_23

Free-Space-Optical Quantum Key Distribution Systems: Challenges and Trends

Josue Aaron Lopez-Leyva, Ariana Talamantes-Alvarez, Miguel A. Ponce-Camacho, Edith Garcia-Cardenas and Eduardo Alvarez-Guzman

Abstract

Nowadays, high security levels are required to transmit critical information for government, private and personal sectors. As a countermeasure, the Quantum Key Distribution systems are the best option in order to protect this information because it provides unconditional security. In addition, increasing the transmission distance is a highlight. Therefore, the Free-Space Optical Quantum Key Distribution systems (FSO-QKD) present an innovative way for sharing secure information between two parties located at ground stations, spacecraft or aircraft. However, these scenarios present several challenges regarding the hardware, protocols and techniques used that must be solved in order to enhance the performance parameters (security level, distance link, final secret key rate, among others) for any QKD system; although, in particular, a high transmission performance is required for both the classical and quantum channels. These issues impose the roadmap and trends in the research, academic and manufacturing sectors around the world.

Keywords: performance parameters, secret key, challenges, trends, Quantum Key Distribution

1. Introduction

Currently, crucial information is shared between two parties located either near or far, in the quantum cryptographic context, the transmitter and receiver side are called Alice and Bob, respectively. Therefore, Alice transmits to Bob important information that requires a high secrecy level based on different kind of cryptography systems against a spy system called Eve. In particular, the most secure systems in the practice and theoretically secure are the Quantum Key Distribution (QKD) systems implemented on fiber optical networks and/or Free Space Optics (FSO) links using both Continuous-Variable (CV) and Discrete-Variable (DV) due to they are based on the physics laws [1]. In general, any QKD system requires on the Alice side different "subsystems" such as optical source, quantum state preparation (QSP), modulation scheme (Mod-Sch) and a Digital Processor & Communication (DP&Comm), among other possible subsystems that can improve the overall performance (**Figure 1**). In particular, the optical source has some important physical and technical requirements that affects the security level; these parameters are the linewidth, quantum optical state generated by the source, wavelength stability, among others. The QSP subsystem is probably the most important subsystem because it intends to prepare a true and well-knowledge quantum state that will be used for encoding the key, that is, to ensure the generation and fidelity features of the quantum state, although some QKD systems impose these requirements to an optimum optical source selection. Regarding the DP&Comm subsystem, many classical technologies are used for digital processing (e.g. central processing unit (CPU), graphical processing unit (GPU), field programmable gate array (FPGA)) in order to implement the algorithm for controlling Mod-Sch subsystem and perform a distillation algorithm for each particular protocol used in QKD systems. On the other hand, the DP&Comm also uses classical telecommunication techniques (e.g. Radio frequency, fiber optics link, FSO links, copper transmission lines) based on a classical and public transmission channel. In addition, the Mod-Sch subsystem uses the output signal of the QSP in order to modify some characteristics (e.g. polarization, amplitude, phase, among others) according to the driving output signal of the DP&Comm. After that, the quantum state that carries information is transmitted through a quantum private channel (fiber optics or free space). At the Bob's side, an optical receiver with support of many optical passive devices receives the quantum optical state and, thus, generates an electrical output signal that will be fed to a demodulation scheme (Demod-Sch). In this case, Bob also has a DP&Comm subsystem with the same characteristics and similar tasks in comparison with the used in Alice.

In addition, Quantum State Determination/Performance Parameters (QSP/PP) subsystem is used for: (a) determining the optical quantum state received by Bob based on optical tomography or calculating the density matrix, or, (b) measuring some important performance parameters of the quantum state received, such as amplitude, phase, polarization, among others, without reconstructing the phase representation state or the density matrix. There exist many subsystems that can improve the performance of QKD systems according to specific conditions, however, this chapter only mentions the most important ones based on authors opinion. On the other hand, Eve system also needs different subsystems in order to "listen" the information from Alice and Bob systems. Therefore, in order to reach the secure level imposed by the physical laws, high-end technology is required in each subsystem mentioned concerning hardware (i.e. subsystems mentioned), protocols, novel materials among others highlight topics [2].

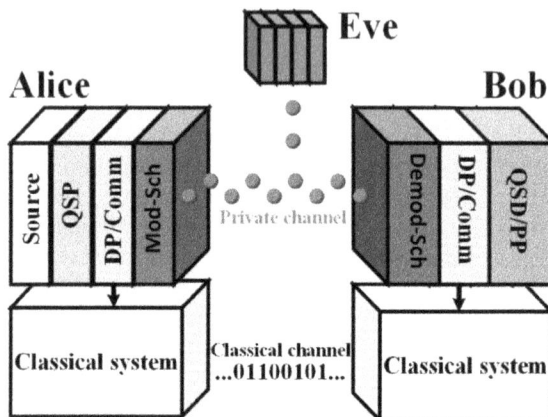

Figure 1.
General block diagram of QKD system emphasizing in the subsystems required for both quantum and classical channel.

Therefore, this chapter explains the state-of-art and actual challenges of each subsystem and devices used in QKD systems for both classical and quantum communications involved in this kind of secure systems. The aforementioned information can help to the reader to visualize and establish a general roadmap of the technologies used in QKD systems in order to focus institutional activities to research, development and innovation to contribute to the scientific and technical sector around the world. This chapter are organized as follows: Sections 2.1, 2.2 and 2.3 show the state-of-art regarding optical sources, optical detector and digital processing systems, respectively. Sections 2.1.1, 2.2.1 and 2.3.1 describe the actual challenges in each particular subsystem and the scientific and technological trends, emphasizing the FSO applications.

2. High-end hardware: challenges and trends

As mentioned above, although QKD systems are unconditionally secure based on laws of quantum mechanics, it is necessary to understand the technological limit of high-end hardware to increase the research, innovation and development activities in order to reach the theoretical performance of a QKD system step by step. In fact, technical limitations and imperfections in the hardware used gives Eve the opportunity to implement some Side-Channel-Attacks (among other attack kinds) based on the non-idealities.

2.1 Optical sources

The most desired optical source for the technical and scientific sector is the single-photon source or on-demand optical source which emit photons at any arbitrary time related to the transmission rate in a deterministic way (not probabilistic), that is, in an ideal case, 100% for emitted a certain photon and 0% for multiple-photons emitted, among others desired features. Thus, many optical sources intend to be a practical single-photon source based on faint laser pulse concept, however, it is not possible to ensure the amount of photons because the probabilistic analysis was made based on the Poisson distribution of the optical signal. On the other hand, there are other type of sources that try the same, but the difference relies in the theory and experiments used in order to generate a single photon. For example: (a) isolated quantum dot systems based on different material such as GaN, CdSe/ZnS, among others. However, these systems are not suitable for C-optical band (i.e. working from $\approx$340 nm to $\approx$950 nm) where the conventional telecommunication systems (and QKD systems) work and present a low emission efficiency (from $\approx$0.02 to $\approx$0.1) [3, 4]. Although it presents an important feature in single-photon sources, that is the deterministic resolving manner; (b) probabilistic single-photon sources based on Parametric Down-Conversion (PDC) and Four-Wave Mixing implemented in bulk crystals/waveguides and optical fiber, respectively. However, the principal issue is the reduced emission efficiency (from $\approx$ 0.1 to $\approx$ 0.85) although they are higher than the systems mentioned in (a). Obviously, this technical option is different compared to the ideal concept of a single-photon source that expects a perfect emission probability for a unique photon; and (c) faint laser is the most useful technique because it relaxes the design and complexity of the implementation of an experiment in both real and laboratory scenarios. This technique presents an emission efficiency of $\approx$1 and a wide inherent bandwidth suitable for the immersion of QKD systems in the real optical networks [4].

Thus, for all the optical sources mentioned, the efficiency and non-linear optical elements are an important issue for design and manufacturing. It is also important to remember that the optical sources described have to be suitable for FSO links where a complete QKD system is implemented, that is, the restriction of single-photon is crucial for support the secure aspect inherent in QKD systems, however, the FSO links imposes trade-off that have to be analyzed. For this reason, the faint pulse is the common technique for FSO applications. Until now, the single-photon source information presented has been analyzed based on certain particular characteristics. However, an important aspect is the quantum state of the single photon generated by the optical source, that is, a photon can be generated with a particular quantum state (related to a quasi-probabilistic density functions) such as coherent, Fock, entanglement, among others. In fact, an ideal single-photon deterministic source should be generating a single photon with Fock distribution. On the other hand, an entanglement "single-photon" (probabilistic way) can be used in some short-distance-FSO-QKD systems and laboratory considering a high efficiency channel and finally, a single-photon source with coherent state (faint laser) is the most useful source and distribution used for long distance free space links.

2.1.1 Challenges and trends

In general, the challenges in the actual optical sources are regarding the band telecommunication of the device, inherent bandwidth, emission efficiency and output spatial mode. Therefore, the important advance imposes a clear trend based on efficient optical sources at common telecom wavelengths (i.e. C-band) [5]. Although sources at O-band are available [6]. Basically, the improved performance of the optical sources is based on the use of novel materials, structures and quantum devices that permits the near-ideal quantum state generation [7].

2.2 Optical detector

An ideal single-photon detector is useful in QKD systems in order to detect and resolve (determinate) an amount of photons per observation time (related to bit), that is, the detector is enabled to detect a single-photon and determine the exact quantity of a single-photon. However, this definition is based on the assumption of an ideal single-photon source. Obviously, ideal single-photon source and detector permits directly assure specific security levels based on the detection of an Eve system that disturbs the amount of photons transmitted by Alice. However, due to physical characteristics of the materials used on the manufacturing, there are deviations between the idealistic and realistic performance parameters. Thus, many realistic single-photon detectors have the ability of distinguish between zero photons per bit and more than zero photons, but they do not resolve the amount of photon. Based on the above, the most common used single-photon detectors are the non-photon-number-resolving detectors, that is, they have the ability of detecting photon but do not resolving the exact amount of photons. However, there are different modes of operation based on multiple detectors that allow improving the resolving process. Some examples about single-photon detector proposals are: (a) the Photo-Multiplier Tube (PMT) which is a classical single-photon detector that operates from the visible region to the infrared. However, the detection efficiency is considerably reduced, for example, at 500 nm the efficiency is 0.4, while for 1550 nm is 0.02; meaning a major problem for its application in some real optical networks; (b) Single-Photon Avalanche Photodiode (SPAP) category has a wide variety of technical options for detection process, having minimum and maximum efficiencies from 0.40 to 0.74 for 450–780 nm band, respectively (based on Silice). In both cases (i.e. a and b options), the wavelength range is not completely suitable for FSO communications systems, although some beacon systems can use these detectors with previous analysis.

Therefore, SPAP based on InGaAs material is suitable for 1060–1550 nm range with maximum efficiency of $\approx$0.33 for 1060 nm and $\approx$0.10 at 1550 nm. Regarding the high-end technology, the superconducting Transition Edge Sensor (TES) is the best option for detecting in FSO-QKD system context based on the detection efficiency-wavelength relationship, that is, efficiency of $\approx$0.95 at 1556 nm. However, the operation temperature is extremely low, $\approx$0.1°K, whereas the last mentioned detectors work commonly from 240 to 300°K, although there are some exceptions [4].

2.2.1 Challenges and trends

The principal challenges are related to minimizing the electronic noise and maximizing the gain of the detector maintaining high transmission rates [8, 9]. To do the aforementioned, novel materials and electrical designs are required. In particular, reducing the Noise Equivalent Power (NEP) parameter permits the detection of low optical power with different electrical bandwidth [10]. However, although novel optical detectors have been developed, coherent detection techniques have been helps at Bob side, relaxing the detector selection due to inherent amplification and spectrum filtering of the coherent technique.

2.3 Digital processing systems

The DP&Comm subsystem implemented in conventional QKD systems performs particular basic tasks such as: driver for different devices (e.g. phase and amplitude modulators, true random number generator (TRNG), etc.), quantum key data base, perform the algorithm need to distillation, reconciliation and privacy amplification processes between Alice and Bob. In particular, this algorithm requires access to both quantum and classical channels. Therefore, the DP&Comm requires some important technical specifications so as not to degrade the secure level and secrete key rate of the QKD systems. In particular, Field Programmable Gate Arrays (FPGA) have been used in a real-time QKD systems reaching secret key rate at 17 kb/s in an optical fiber link of 20 Km [11]. It is clear that, the FPGA specifications impact the performance of a QKD systems, therefore, improved synchronization and jitter methods based on high speed and precision devices can reduce the Quantum Bit Error Rate (QBER) and increase the final secret key rate [12].

In addition, the secret key rate has an important relation with the performance of the TRNG subsystems, thus, FPGAs have been used for generation and acquisition of true random digital sequences reaching 1.25 Gb/s [13]. An important issue in DP&Comm subsystems is the ability to adapt and generate countermeasures to maintain or improve the specific performance against external dynamic factors such as atmospheric turbulence in FSO links, resizing and adaptive parameters based on an optimization process [14, 15]. In addition, some QKD systems use a Graphics Processing Unit (GPU) as a DP&Comm (although some considerations have to be analyzed to complete all the task of the DP&Comm) because it provides some important technical features such as parallel computing and processing floating-point information allowing rates of 1.35 Gb/s [16]. The novel standalone modules for particular stages of the protocol used (e.g. sifting, error correction, and privacy amplification modules) also support the performance of QKD systems, which are based on high-end electronic design. These particular technical innovations in specific modules permits reaching secret key rate of $\approx$13.72 Mb/s [17].

2.3.1 Challenges and trends

Thus, the DP&Comm subsystem depends on the electronic development regarding the high performance related to speed processing and the novel design of Printed Circuit Board (PCB) used in different subsystems within DP&Comm. Among the devices that need to be improved are high-end converters (Digital-to-Analog-Converter and Analog-to-Digital-Converter), fast output/input ports (e.g. analog and digital) and fast memories. On the other hand, an optimized QKD protocol have to be programmed in DP&Comm subsystems, which includes different algorithms needed in different protocol stages, that is, detecting-correcting errors codes, performing some Hash functions among other used. Therefore, no matter the high-end devices used in the DP&Comm subsystem, the designer should try to reduce the trade-off based on optimized programming.

In addition, Commercial Off-The-Shelf (COTS) devices have been used for QKD-FSO systems using an optimized protocol to not degrade the security level and secret key rate [18]. **Figures 2** and 3 show the Alice and Bob set-up, respectively. Both systems use COTS devices in a Local Area Network (LNA). In particular, Alice set up (**Figure 2**) consists of an optical source in order to generate a LO and a data signal (the way to divide the optical signal is not graphically clear expressed, but 1X2 fiber splitters were used), the LO signal will be sent to Bob separately in order to perform a self-homodyne detection. In addition, a minimum optical signal is used for the TRNG to generate two random digital sequences (RSA1 and RSA2). These sequences are used by a COTS device that uses a DB-RN in order to drive the PM and perform the quantum protocol using both classical and quantum channels. The PC and PBS are used in order to maintain and ensure a vertical SOP in the incoming PM signal because in order to avoid a residual amplitude modulation. Since the optical source is non-polarized and it has an optical fiber output, a PC is used as the first element for polarization controlling, but because Alice and Bob have to be implemented in free space, a PBS was added in order to ensure the SOP. However, the PC can be deleted if an optical source with free space coupling and linear vertical polarization is used. Thus, residual amplitude modulation can affect the overall performance of the QKD systems. Next, phase modulation is used to encrypt the information and a half-wave plate to produce a linear SOP at 45 degrees needed for Bob set-up. Because the optical source generates a coherent state, an attenuator is used to produce a weak coherent state emulating a long distance free-space link. Before the optical signal is transmitted through the free space channel, a BS and PD are used for monitoring the optical power corresponding to the weak coherent state.

At the Bob side (**Figure 3**), a free space optical hybrid (π-hybrid) based on BS, PBS and BHDs is used in order to measure simultaneously both quadrature components of the weak coherent stated received. Mirrors and attenuators are used in order to calibrate the optical power received in each photodetector (implemented in each BHDs) due to the different optical paths. In particular, a quarter-wave plate

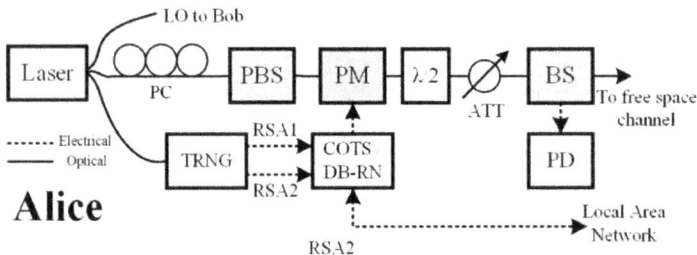

Figure 2.
Alice set-up. PBS, polarized beam splitter; TRNG, true random number generator; PM, phase modulator; DB-RN, database-random number; BS, beam splitter; ATT, attenuator; PD, photodetector; RSA, random sequence in Alice; PC, polarization controller; λ/2, half-wave plate; LO, local oscillator. Own figure and presented in [18].

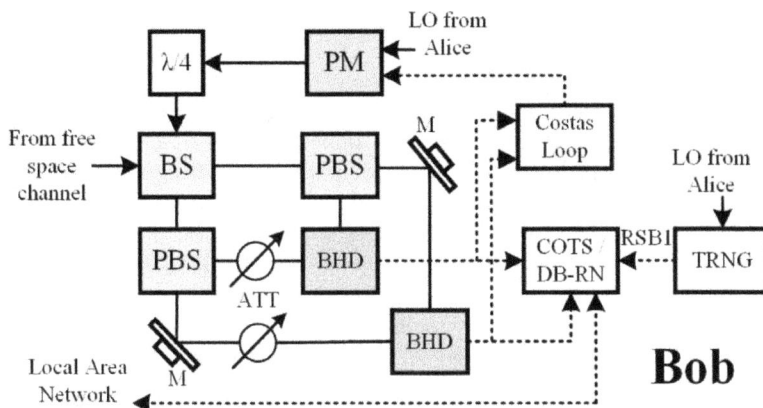

Figure 3.
Bob set-up. M, mirror; BHD, balanced homodyne detector; λ/4, quarter-wave plate; RSB, random sequence in bob. Own figure and presented in [18].

is used to change the SOP of the LO, that is, the LO needs a circular SOP in order to allow simultaneous measurements. Therefore, the complete Bob scheme is based on coherent detection technique, where an opto-electronic Costal loop permits the improvement of the complete performance reducing the phase noise due to different optical paths. Particularly, a COTS device and TRNG (it generates other random digital sequence, RSB1) are used in a similar way as Alice in order to perform the quantum protocol. The quantum transmitter-receiver shows an experimental average Quantum Bit Error Rate (QBER) of 30% using auto-homodyne detection with 0.25 photons per bit in locking phase mode. The final secret key rate measurements were 20 and 40 Kbps for minimum and maximum throughput in the LAN. Finally, although common elements (i.e. passive and active optical elements) are used in **Figures 2** and **3**, the important aspect is the uses of COTS devices in QKD systems that allow relaxing some design parameters maintain adequate performance parameters as mentioned (e.g. QBER, final secret key rate).

3. QKD protocols: challenges and trends

The research on the protocols used for the distribution of the cryptographic key based on the principles of quantum mechanics had a great boom in the last 10 years. In general, the QKD protocols describe the particular tasks or steps (i.e. algorithm) needed in order to generate a final quantum secret key rate. Although the QKD protocols are programmed in a DP&Comm subsystem, they require all the subsystems. In particular, the protocols and their performance depend on the statistical information (discrete and continuous variables, DV and CV, respectively) regarding the quantum state used.

The BB84 protocol is the first protocol proposed to guarantee unconditional security (because it is based on orthogonal states) when transmitting the cryptographic key that gives access to the information of a message. It has been considered as the ideal protocol, at least in theory, since it is based on the transmission of the quantum state of a single photon to represent a bit of information and provide immediate information through the characteristics of the received signal, about a possible attack by a spy [19]. In addition, if we add that the key is used in a single occasion (One Time Pad) it provides better protection in case that at some point an intruder manages to obtain the key. Next, B92 protocol was proposed based on BB84 protocol.

While BB84 protocol uses 4 orthogonal states, B92 only uses 2 non-orthogonal states. Therefore, the different quantum states (i.e. orthogonal and non-orthogonal) used in BB84 and B92 protocols impose a trade-off regarding the final secret key rate generated by Alice, Bob and the attacks performed by Eve [20]. Since the BB84 protocol is extremely vulnerable to Photon Number Splitting attacks, the SARG04 protocol was proposed, which uses 4 non-orthogonal quantum states; however, the final secret key rate is also affected [21]. Additionally, there exists the E91 protocol based on Einstein, Podolsky and Rosen (EPR) paradox that uses entangled quantum states generated either by Alice, Bob or a trusted third party [22]. Later, the BBM92 protocol was proposed which implies EPR pairs, that is, entangled photon pairs. This protocol can be described as the BB84-EPR protocol [23]. Until now, the protocols mentioned are based on State of Polarization (SOP), DV framework and general stages such as: raw key exchange, key sifting and privacy amplification, that is, all the protocols have the same stages in order to generate the final quantum key. On the other hand, QKD protocols based on CV variables are also suitable, such as COW protocol (Coherent One-Way), which is based on an amplitude encoded sequence of weak coherent pulse with the same phase for each particular time slot. In particular, different time slots have several optical pulses (related to an optical power average) and, occasionally, decoy sequences are sent in order to hinder the eavesdropped process [24]. Due to the different quantum states and encoding scheme used, this protocol is so-called distributed-phase-reference (DPR), in fact, there are many protocols in the same category such as the differential-phase-shift (DPS), which uses different phases but the amplitude remains constant. Therefore, interferometric techniques are required in the receiver [25]. All the DPR protocols perform joint measurements on subsequent signals. Actually, GG02 protocol is present in many commercial equipment. In general, this protocol is based on random distributions of coherent or squeezed states and modulates either the phase or amplitude of a quantum state and uses coherent detection in Bob's side [26]. Finally, each protocol mentioned has a particular security principle, be it the Heisenberg uncertainty or quantum entanglement. Although there exist novel protocols that change the security principle in order to improve the performance of particular QKD systems.

3.1 Challenges and trends

The challenges present in the QKD protocols are related with the performance parameters of the QKD systems. In particular, although each protocol uses different security principle and quantum states, the important issues are increasing the security level, secret key rate and distance link between Alice and Bob in presence of Eve system. In fact, while a particular protocol presents a high security level and particular secret key rate for short distance links, other protocol presents the same security level and secret key rate for long distance links. However, as was mentioned, a QKD protocol requires the other subsystems, thus, a hypothetically complicated protocol imposes a strict and detailed design, that is, the experimental set-up is not simple. Therefore, the tendency of the protocols refers to proposing novel QKD protocols that allow to easily implement them in optical commercial networks, while the performance parameters remain constant or improved. In addition, a high dimension protocol is proposed in order to increase the photon information capacity when the photon rate is restrained. This protocol is based on entangled photon pairs that allow information to be transmitted using an extremely large alphabet [27].

Now, each QKD protocol has been theoretically described, however, free space and atmospheric channels impose important trade-off that determines the suitable protocol. In particular, BB84 protocol has been optimized for FSO links affected by atmospheric turbulence improving the secret key rate up to over 20% [28].

However, BB84 protocol remains unchanged while other subsystems are modified. In fact, many QKD protocols have been implemented in FSO links in order to demonstrate their performance under particular conditions.

4. Techniques and structure in QKD: challenges and trends

The techniques and structures used in QKD context involve the different set-ups, operation rules and devices that perform a particular protocol. Therefore, the first step is choosing the quantum protocol and next, the general structure can be proposed and implemented. In particular, the structure consists of optical source, optical detector, digital processing unit (the challenges and trends that have already been mentioned) among other specific devices connected together in order to perform a complete QKD system. On the other hand, the techniques are the novel operational rules in order to enhance the complete performance of the QKD system. Each protocol mentioned was proofed, first, using a particular technique and structure, these can be can be found and analyzed in the references listed. However, many improves to each protocol have been proposed for QKD systems implemented in FSO.

For example, the atmospheric turbulence is an important problem for QKD systems based on FSO links. In order to mitigate the degraded performance of the secret key rate for QKD systems based on BB84 protocol, an optimization technique was proposed based on an adaptive optical power transmission considering the random irradiance fluctuation [28]. In the same context, a novel encoder technique was proposed for the classical channel in QKD-FSO systems based on adaptively encoder gain according to atmospheric turbulence levels [29], The results show that the secret key rate remains constant for a region of turbulence levels and imposes the need of a high-end DP&Comm subsystem in order to extend the operating region. In addition, many structures and techniques used in conventional classical optical communication systems have been adapted to QKD-FSO systems. In particular, Multi-Input-Multi-Output (MIMO) and Wavelength Division Multiplexing (WDM) are suitable options used in order to increase the capacity of free space channel based on Orthogonal Angular Momentum (OAM) modulation [30]. Among the structures and techniques necessary to implement a QKD-FSO system are the subsystems used in order to pointing, acquisition and tracking the two parties (Alice and Bob, represented by satellites and ground stations). In this case, pointing systems used in satellites have reached from 0.6 μrad to 3 μrad pointing capability [31, 32].

4.1 Challenges and trends

In general, the structures and techniques allow to improve the performance of a QKD-FSO system. Therefore, the design of techniques and high-end structures allows to support in a better way the actual QKD system proposals. In fact, the principal challenges are related with the optimization and improving of the secondary subsystems of a QKD-FSO systems (i.e. secondary subsystems are not mentioned in detail in this chapter, such as telescope, mechanical structures, access multiplexing techniques, among others). Finally, the QKD-FSO system trends related with the structures and techniques are: maximize the channel capacity, increase the distance link and secret key rate, increase the power consumption efficiency in order to support long-time missions, improve the thermal control and isolation, among others.

In addition, novel encoding technique for classical channel has been proposed in order to increase the secret key rate at QKD-FSO links. **Figure 4** shows a diagram proposed based on an adaptive LDPC (Low-Density Parity-Check Codes) encoder in order to countermeasure the effect caused by the dynamical atmospheric turbulence [29].

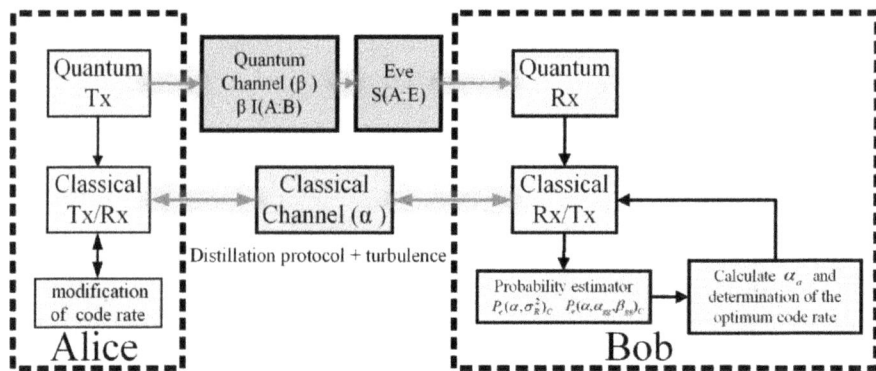

Figure 4.
Block diagram of the simulation-experimental set-up of the QKD system proposed with dynamical encoder for different atmospheric turbulence levels. Own figure and presented in [29].

Here, $I(A{:}B)$ is the mutual information that Alice and Bob shared, and the maximum information shared for Alice and Eve is $S(A{:}E)$. In this case, β_{gg} is the reconciliation efficiency. In other hand, α is the classical channel efficiency that is based on the encoder capacity (related to the amount the erroneous bits that are detected and corrected). In this scenario, the dynamical atmospheric turbulence is represented by Rayleigh or Gamma-Gamma (GG) density probability functions, $P_e(\alpha,\sigma_R^2)_c$ and $P_e(\alpha,\alpha_{gg},\beta_{gg})_c$, respectively, where σ_R^2 represents the Rytov variance related with the atmospheric turbulence, α_{gg} and β_{gg} are the effective numbers of large-scale and small-scale for GG function, respectively. Basically, Alice and Bob monitored the dynamical atmospheric turbulence calculating the error probabilities and modifying LDPC encoder capacity used by them.

5. Conclusions

The proper understanding of the high-end hardware, protocols, techniques and schemes used in FSO-QKD systems allow to improve the performance parameters such as secret key rate, distance link, security level, among others. In particular, although there are wide suitable options for the subsystems required for FSO-QKD systems, it is necessary that the high-end subsystems are more accessible and compact in order to increase their uses in traditional optical networks.

Acknowledgements

Many thanks to CETYS University for the administrative and technical support in the development of diverse projects related to the subject mentioned in this chapter. In addition, thanks to the Center of Innovation and Design (CEID) of Baja California for the important discussion on improving quality of the chapter.

Author details

Josue Aaron Lopez-Leyva[1*], Ariana Talamantes-Alvarez[1],
Miguel A. Ponce-Camacho[1], Edith Garcia-Cardenas[2] and
Eduardo Alvarez-Guzman[3]

1 CETYS University, Baja California, Mexico

2 IBERO University, Baja California, Mexico

3 Autonomous University of Baja California, Baja California, Mexico

*Address all correspondence to: josue.lopez@cetys.mx

IntechOpen

References

[1] Qu Z, Djordjevic IB. High-speed free-space optical continuous-variable quantum key distribution enabled by three-dimensional multiplexing. Optics Express. 2017;**25**:7919-7928. DOI: 10.1364/OE.25.007919

[2] Diamanti E, Lo H-K, Qi B, Yuan Z. Practical challenges in quantum key distribution. npj Quantum Information. 2016;**2**:1-12. DOI: 10.1038/npjqi.2016.25

[3] Schlehahn A, Fischbach S, Schmidt R, Kaganskiy A, Strittmatter A, Rodt S, et al. A stand-alone fiber-coupled single-photon source. Scientific Reports. 2018;**8**:1-7. DOI: 10.1038/s41598-017-19049-4

[4] Eisaman MD, Fan J, Migdall A, Polyakov SV. Invited review article: Single-photon sources and detectors. Review of Scientific Instruments. 2011;**82**:1-26. DOI: 10.1063/1.3610677

[5] Haffouz S, Zeuner KD, Dalacu D, Poole PJ, Lapointe J, Poitras D, et al. Bright single InAsP quantum dots at telecom wavelengths in position-controlled InP nanowires: The role of the photonic waveguide. Nano Letters. 2018;**18**:3047-3052. DOI: 10.1021/acs.nanolett.8b00550

[6] Dusanowski L, Holewa P, Maryński A, Musiał A, Heuser T, Srocka N, et al. Triggered high-purity telecom-wavelength single-photon generation from p-shell-driven InGaAs/GaAs quantum dot. Optics Express. 2017;**25**:31122-31129. DOI: 10.1364/OE.25.031122

[7] Heindel T, Rodt S, Reitzenstein S. Single-photon sources based on deterministic quantum-dot microlenses. In: Michler P, editor. Quantum Dots for Quantum Information Technologies. Springer; 2017. pp. 199-228. DOI: 10.1007/978-3-319-56378-7

[8] Abdulwahid OS, Sexton J, Kostakis I, Ian K, Missous M. Physical modelling and experimental characterisation of InAlAs/InGaAs avalanche photodiode for 10 Gb/s data rates and higher. IET Optoelectronics. 2018;**12**:5-10. DOI: 10.1049/iet-opt.2017.0068

[9] Tossoun B, Stephens R, Wang Y, Addamane S, Balakrishnan G, Holmes A, et al. High-speed InP-based p-i-n photodiodes with InGaAs/GaAsSb type-II quantum wells. Photonics Technology Letters. 2018;**30**:399-402. DOI: 10.1109/LPT.2018.2793663

[10] Jiang X, Itzler M, O'Donnell K, Entwistle M, Owens M, Slomkowski K, et al. InP-based single-photon detectors and Geiger-mode APD arrays for quantum communications applications. Journal of Selected Topics in Quantum Electronics. 2015;**21**:3800112. DOI: 10.1109/JSTQE.2014.2358685

[11] Zhang H-F, Wang J, Cui K, Luo C-L, Lin S-Z, Zhou L, et al. A real-time QKD system based on FPGA. Journal of Lightwave Technology. 2012;**30**:3226-3234. DOI: 10.1109/JLT.2012.2217394

[12] Shen Q, Liao S, Liu S, Wang J, Liu W, Peng C, et al. An FPGA-based TDC for free space quantum key distribution. Transactions on Nuclear Science. 2013;**60**:3570-3577. DOI: 10.1109/TNS.2013.2280169

[13] Martin A, Sanguinetti B, Wen Lim CC, Houlmann R, Zbinden H. Quantum random number generation for 1.25-GHz quantum key distribution systems. Journal of Lightwave Technology. 2015;**33**:2855-2859. DOI: 10.1109/JLT.2015.2416914

[14] Yang S-S, Bai Z-L, Wang X-Y, Li Y-M. FPGA-based implementation of size-adaptive privacy amplification in quantum key distribution. Photonics

Journal. 2017;**9**:1-8. DOI: 10.1109/
JPHOT.2017.2761807

[15] Yan Z, Meyer-Scott E, Bourgoin
J-P, Higgins B-L, Gigov N, Mac Donald
A, et al. Novel high-speed polarization
source for decoy-state BB84 quantum
key distribution over free space and
satellite links. Lightwave Technology.
2013;**31**:1399-1408. DOI: 10.1109/
JLT.2013.2249040

[16] Wang X, Zhang Y, Yu S, Guo
H. High-speed implementation
of length-compatible privacy
amplification in continuous-variable
quantum key distribution. Photonics
Journal. 2018;**10**:1-9. DOI: 10.1109/
JPHOT.2018.2824316

[17] Yuan Z, Plews A, Takahashi R, Doi
K, Tam W, Sharpe A, et al. 10-Mb/s
quantum key distribution. Journal of
Lightwave Technology. 2018;**36**:3427-
3433. DOI: 10.1109/JLT.2018.2843136

[18] Lopez-Leyva JA, Ruiz-Higuera J,
Arvizu-Mondragon A, Santos-Aguilar
J, Ramos-Garcia R, Ponce-Camacho
M. High performance quantum
key distribution prototype system
using a commercial off-the-shelf
solution: Experimental and emulation
demonstrations. Optica Applicata.
2017;**XLVII**:411-419. DOI: 10.5277/
oa170307

[19] Bennet CH, Brassard G. Quantum
cryptography: Public key distribution
and coin tossing. Theoretical Computer
Science. 2014;**560**:7-11. DOI: 10.1016/j.
tcs.2014.05.025

[20] Bennett CH. Quantum
cryptography using any two non-
orthogonal states. Physical Review
Letters. 1992;**68**:3121-3124. DOI:
10.1103/PhysRevLett.68.3121

[21] Scarani V, Acín A, Ribordy G,
Gisin N. Quantum cryptography
protocols robust against photon number

splitting attacks for weak laser pulse
implementations. Physical Review
Letters. 2004;**92**:057901. DOI: 10.1103/
PhysRevLett.92.057901

[22] Artur E. Quantum cryptography
based on Bell's theorem. Physical Review
Letters. 1991;**67**:661-663. DOI: 10.1103/
PhysRevLett.67.661

[23] Bennett CH, Brassard G, Mermin
ND. Quantum cryptography without
Bell's theorem. Physical Review
Letters. 1992;**68**:557-559. DOI: 10.1103/
PhysRevLett.68.557

[24] Stucki D, Brunner N, Gisin
N, Scarani V, Zbinden H. Fast
and simple one-way quantum key
distribution. Applied Physics Letters.
2005;**87**:194108. DOI: 10.1063/1.2126792

[25] Inoue K, Waks E, Yamamoto
Y. Differential-phase-shift quantum
key distribution using coherent light.
Physical Review A. 2003;**68**:022317.
DOI: 10.1103/PhysRevA.68.022317

[26] Grosshans F, Grangier P. Continuous
variable quantum cryptography using
coherent states. Physical Review
Letters. 2002;**88**:057902. DOI: 10.1103/
PhysRevLett.88.057902

[27] Bechmann-Pasquinucci H, Tittel
W. Quantum cryptography using
larger alphabets. Physical Review
A. 2000;**61**:062308. DOI: 10.1103/
PhysRevA.61.062308

[28] Sun X, Djordjevic IB, Neifeld
MA. Secret key rates and optimization
of BB84 and decoy state protocols
over time-varying free-space
optical channels. Photonics Journal.
2016;**8**:7904713. DOI: 10.1109/
JPHOT.2016.2570000

[29] Lopez-Leyva JA, Arvizu-
Mondragon A, Santos-Aguilar J, Ramos-
Garcia R. Improved performance of
the cryptographic key distillation
protocol of an FSO/CV-QKD system on

a turbulent channel using an adaptive
LDPC encoder. Revista Mexicana de
Fisica. 2017;**63**:268-274

[30] Cvijetic M, Takashima Y. Beyond
1Mb/s free-space optical quantum
key distribution. In: Proceedings of
the IEEE International Conference
on Transparent Optical Networks
(ICTON'14). Graz, Austria: IEEE; 6-10
July 2014. pp. 1-4

[31] Yin J et al. Satellite-based
entanglement distribution over 1200
kilometers. Science. 2017;**356**:1140-
1144. DOI: 10.1126/science.aan3211

[32] Oi DKL et al. Cube Sat quantum
communications mission. EPJ Quantum
Technology. 2017;**4**:1-20. DOI: I 10.1140/
epjqt/s40507-017-0060-1

Chapter 4

Coherence Proprieties of Entangled Bi-Modal Field and Its Application in Holography and Communication

Nicolae A. Enaki

Abstract

This chapter examines the coherence properties of two modes of entangled photons and its application quantum communication and holography. It is proposed novel two-photon entangled sources which take into account the coherence and collective phenomena between the photon belonging to two different modes obtained in two-photon cooperative emission or Raman or lasing. The generation of the correlated bimodal entangled field in two-photon emission or Raman Pump, Stokes and anti-Stokes modes is proposed in the free space and cavity-induced emission. The application two-photon and Raman bimodal coherent field in communication and holography are given in accordance with the definition of amplitude and phase of such entangled states of light. At first, this method does not appear to be essentially different in comparison with the classical coherent state of information processing, but if we send this information in dispersive media, which separates the anti-Stokes and Stokes photons from coherent entanglement fields, the information is drastically destroyed, due to the quantum distribution of photons in the big number modes may be realized in the situation in which the mean value of strength of bimodal field tends to zero. The possibility of restoration of the signal after the propagation of the bimodal field through different fibers, we may restore the common square amplitude and phase.

Keywords: quantum bimodal field, cooperative effects between blocks of photons, quantum communication, quantum holography

1. Introduction in the specific properties of correlated bimodal radiation field

Generated radiation in two- or multi-quantum processes opens new perspectives in studying new communication systems, holographic phase correlations, in the interaction of light with biomolecules and living systems. The specific attention is given to the new type of coherent emissions, which occurs not only between the quantum but between the photon groups generated in the non-linear interaction of the electromagnetic field (EMF) with emitters (atoms, molecules, biomolecules, etc.). This type of light generation supports the idea of coherent correlation that appears in the bi-modal field, in which it is generated the entangled photons.

A physical characteristic of field formed from the blocs of well-correlated bi-modes must be determined by the intensity of the electric field of each mode characteristic in such superposition. The applications of such a field characteristic can be fruitful both in quantum communication and holography. An attractive aspect of the problem consists in the selective two-quantum excitation of some atoms or molecules of the system, where it is necessary minimize the dipole active action of total photon flux over single-photon resonance of dipole-active transitions. The last idea can be applied in microbiology, where a selective dis-activation of some molecular structures (e.g. of viruses) in the tissue may become possible in two-quanta excitations. In this situation appears the necessity for a good description of both amplitude and phase of this new type of radiation formed from bimodal correlated photons.

The new concept of phase and amplitude correlations are important not only in interferometry but also in the holographic registration of information and are related to the conceptual aspects of physics, chemistry and microbiology for the recording of three and multi-dimensional images in cosmology [1–3]. According to the invention of Dennis Gabor [4] in 1947, the hologram is defined by the interference between two waves, the 'object wave' and the 'reference wave'. Like in laser experiments, this interference between the two waves requires to use the temporally and spatially consistent source, described by an intensity pattern, which represents the modulus squared of the sum of the two complex amplitudes. The reconstruction of the object field encoded within the hologram is based on the principle of light diffraction. This type of diffraction and interference can be keyed out by other coherent states, which can be an eigenstate of square parts of positive frequency strength of EMF. According to this description, the eigenvalue of vectors of square strength has the good amplitude and phase. For example, in the two photon cooperative emission by the pencil shape system of radiators (or by the cavity two-photon induced emission) the coherence is based between the photon pairs rather than between the individual photons. This effect is evident, when the pairs of photons are generated in the broadband spectral region of the EMF so, that the total energy of two photons in each pair is constant $2\hbar\omega_0 = \hbar\omega_{k1} + \hbar\omega_{k2} = Const.$ Considering that the frequencies of the photons in the pairs are aleatory distributed, $\omega_{ki} \neq \omega_{kj}$, we conclude that such systems generates the higher the second order coherence relative to first order one. In this context appear the problem of the application of such field in communication and holography, using its good amplitude and phase of squared strength, generated by the nominated sources. This chapter discusses the problem associated with the possibilities to divide the wave front of the photon-pairs into two wave fronts. Studying the interference between each part, "object bimodal waves" $\hat{E}^+(t+\tau)\hat{E}^+(t+\tau)$ and "reference bimodal waves" $\hat{E}^+(t)\hat{E}^+(t)$, we may create the hologram image consisted of the interference and diffraction fringes between the bi-photons belonging to wave fronts of square vectors of field consisted from the ensemble of bi-modal field, $\langle\hat{E}^+(t+\tau)\hat{E}^+(t+\tau)\hat{E}^-(t)\hat{E}^-(t)\rangle$.

To understood this type of coherence let us look at the light that consists of distinctive photons, which belong to broadband spectrum energy. Since the number of modes is relatively large, it is virtually impossible to find the two photons in the same mode and to create the coherent states from them, $\langle\hat{E}_k^-(t,z)\hat{E}_{k'}^+(t,z)\rangle \approx 0$, where $\hat{E}_k^-(t,z)$ and $\hat{E}_{k'}^+(t,z)$ is the Fourier transform the negative or positive defined EMF strength components of the radiation modes $k \neq k'$ obtained from the inverted atomic ensemble in z direction. Of course, the total intensity of such a light, obtained from individual sources (nuclei, atoms, molecules) becomes proportional to the number of atomic sources, $I = \sum_j \langle \hat{\mathcal{E}}_j^-(t,z)\hat{\mathcal{E}}_j^+(t,z)\rangle \propto N$, because the correlation function between the strengths of different radiators is $\langle \hat{\mathcal{E}}_j^-(t,z)\hat{\mathcal{E}}_l^+(tz)\rangle|_{l\neq j} \approx 0$. Here $\hat{\mathcal{E}}_j^-(t,z)$ $(\hat{\mathcal{E}}_j^+(t,z))$ is the negative (positive) frequency component of the EMF through of each atom.

The creation of entangled photons in two- and multi-quantum processes opens the new possibilities in quantum communication and quantum holography. For example in the paper of prof. Teich et al. [5] it is proposed to make use of quantum entanglement for extracting holographic information about a remote $3 - D$ object in a confined space which light enters, but from which it cannot escape. Light scattered from the object is detected in this confined space entirely without the benefit of spatial resolution. Quantum holography offers this possibility by virtue of the fourth-order quantum coherence inherent in entangled beams. This new conception is based on the application of second ordered coherence function, proposed firstly by Glauber [6], and intensively developed in the last years. The possibility to use of the fourth-order quantum coherence of entangled beams was studied in Ref. [7]. Here it is proposed a two-photon analog of classical holography. Not so far the authors of Refs. [8, 9] used an innovative equipment registered the behavior of pairs of distinguishable and non-distinguishable photons entering a beam splitter. When the photons are distinguishable, their behavior at the beam splitter is random: one or both photons can be transmitted or reflected. Non-distinguishable photons exhibit quantum interference, which alters their behavior: they join into pairs and are always transmitted or reflected together. This is known as two-photon interference or the Hong-Ou-Mandel effect. The visibility of the hologram of a single photon fringe, V, is defined by a spectral mode overlap which can be high and stable for photons generated by different sources such as two independent spontaneous parametric down-conversion. As the authors mentioned, in the registration of single photon hologram [8], the quantum interference can be observed by registering pairs of photons. The experiment needs to be repeated several times using the two photon pairs with identical properties.

The authors of the Refs. [10-13] have proposed to investigate the coherence which appears between undistinguished photon pairs and the possibility to generate such a pair in the two-photon quantum generators. The increased interest not only to two-photon generation, but to induce Raman microscopy in special medicine and biology opens the new perspective the coherent proprieties of bimodal fields. Compared to spontaneous Raman scattering, coherent Raman scattering techniques can produce much stronger vibrational sensitive signals. This excitation needs a strong phase correlation between the pump, Stokes, and anti-Stokes components of the induced Raman process. These difficulties have been overcome by recent advances in coherent Raman scattering microscopy, which is based on either coherent anti-Stokes Raman scattering or stimulated Raman scattering [14, 15]. Appear a possibility to use this type of coherent states of bimodal field [12, 13], and to propose a new studies of vibrational aspects of molecules.

Following this idea let us discuss another effect related to the photon scattering processes into the pump, Stokes and anti-Stokes modes. Taking into consideration that in the Λ-type three-level system persists only pumping and Stokes modes when the atomic system is prepared in the ground state, or it may be reduced to the pump and anti-Stokes modes, when the atomic system is prepared in the excited state, we could reduce this cooperative scattering effect to the ensemble of correlated pairs of modes in the resonator. This is possible due to big detuning between the third level and pump modes when the system of atoms is prepared in the ground state. In this situation, it is possible to generate m pairs of correlated mods between the pump and Stokes components, so that the frequency difference between the modes of each pair, $\omega_{kp_1} - \omega_{ks_1}$, $\omega_{ks_2} - \omega_{ks_2}$, $\omega_{kp_j} - \omega_{ksj}$, $\omega_{kp_m} - \omega_{ks_m}$ is equal to the transition energy between the ground and excited levels $2\omega_0$. In this description, the pump, and Stokes fields are considered to be incoherent due to the fact that the correlation functions between the pump and Stokes modes, belonging to different partitions gives zero contributions in the intensity correlation function $\langle \hat{E}^{(-)}_{k_{pj}}(t) \hat{E}^{(+)}_{k_{pl}}(t) \rangle_{j \neq l}$ and $\langle \hat{E}^{(-)}_{k_{sj}}(t) \hat{E}^{(+)}_{k_{sl}}(t) \rangle_{j \neq l}$. According to this only the diagonal elements belonging to the same modes remain non-zero so that the field intensity is proportional to this number "m". The resulting intensity of the pumping light is equal to the square strength of each pumping (or Stokes) modes

$$I_p = \sum_j \langle \hat{E}^{(-)}_{k_{pj}}(t) \hat{E}^{(+)}_{k_{pj}}(t) \rangle \sim m \ \text{(or } I_s = \sum_j \langle \hat{E}^{(-)}_{k_{sj}}(t) \hat{E}^{(+)}_{k_{sj}}(t) \rangle \sim m).$$ The realization of

such cooperative effects between the incoherent bi-modes can be obtained exactly as in the case of the two-photon generation in a wide spectrum at Raman emission (e.g., in the multimodal cavity or crossing the pumping pulse through a multimodal optical fiber). The total pumping field strength and Stokes is a multi-mode superposition for both pumping and Stokes mods, where the pumping field and Stokes are decomposed into the quantized states of the optical cavity.

The possibilities of correlations between the anti-Stokes, Stokes and pump modes have been overcome by recent advances in coherent Raman scattering microscopy, which is based on either coherent coherent anti-Stokes Raman scattering or coherent Raman scattering [14, 15]. In many cases, the phase correlations between these components become not so simple in the experimental realization. Appear the possibility to apply here the coherent states of bimodal field proposed in this chapter and a possibility to use holographic aspects of such bimodal field in biology and medicine where the phase and amplitude of Raman component are already correlated for coherent excitation of molecular vibrations

$$\hat{\Pi}^-(t) = \sum_j \hat{E}^{(-)}_{k_{sj}}(t) \hat{E}^{(+)}_{k_{pj}}(t).$$ Here we notice that this new characteristic of the field in

induced Raman process may have a good phase and amplitude as the traditional coherent field, $\Pi^-(t) = \Pi_0 \exp[-i\phi]$, the correlatives between the adjacent modes is proportional to the square number of adjacent bi-mods $\langle \hat{\Pi}^-(t) \hat{\Pi}^+(t) \rangle \sim m^2$. Phase $\phi = 2\omega_0 t - Kz$ contains a fixed frequency $2\omega_0 = \omega_{pki} - \omega_{ski}$ (here $i = 1, 2, ...m$) and a well-defined wave vector, $K = k_{pi} - k_{si}$ in the collinear cavity conversion of the photons from the pump field.

In the Section 2 we give the definition of bimodal coherent states in analogy with single photon coherent states. The definition of phase and amplitude of this bimodal field is also granted, taking into account the coherent states of bimodal superposition of entangled photon pairs and bimodal superposition of Stokes pump and anti-Stokes modes in the Raman scattering process. The lithographic proprieties of such bimodal field are given, taking into consideration multi-mode aspects of generation light.

The Section 3 is devoted to applications of coherent emission of two subgroups of photons, the total (or difference) energies of which can be reckoned as a constant, so that coherence appear between the vectors formed from the product of two electromagnetic field strengths. As it is shown that the coherence between such vectors is manifested if the emitted bi-photons belonging to broadband spectrum, hence that the coherence between individual photons can be neglected. The application of product strength amplitudes and phases in holographic registration is advised. The superposition of two vectors of bimodal field obtained in two-photon or Raman lasing effect is estimated for construction of the holographic image of the object.

2. Generation of biharmonic strength operators and their coherent proprieties

Let us consider two nonlinear processes of light generation in laser [16, 13] and collective decay phenomena [17, 18]. In the second order of interaction of light with matter, these processes strongly connect the quantum fluctuations of two waves. In the output detection region, this effect gives us the possibility to obtain the coherent effects between the bimodal fields as this is proposed in Section 1. In this nonlinear generation of light, the new signal at another frequency has a common coherent phase with impute mode in the nonlinear medium. We discuss the situation when the phases of the emitted waves are random relative to one another so that the total field average of EMF strength takes zero value $\langle \hat{E}(x,t) \rangle = 0$. In such a situation the emission is considered non-coherent. An opposite conception appears in quantum optics in which it is proposed a lot of effects connected with quantum entanglement and coherent proprieties of bimodal field [19]. Here as we discuss in Section 1 we have the possibility to introduce another type of coherence [12, 19, 20], which appear not between the photons of the same mode, but between the biphotons from the ensemble of pairs of modes or correlations of photons belonging to scattered modes (bi-modes) $\langle \hat{E}_r \hat{E}_s \rangle \neq 0$. When the number of bi-modes with the same energy of the photons in the pair increase [21, 22], the quantum fluctuations in each mode may achieve zero value $\langle \hat{E}_r \rangle = \langle \hat{E}_s \rangle = 0$. Following this conception, the similar coherence between the photons we introduced in the Raman emission processes [12, 13, 23]. In this case one photon from non-coherent driving field is absorbed (Stokes photon a_s) and other photon is generated (anti-Stokes b_a^+) $\langle \hat{E}_r \hat{E}_a \rangle \neq 0$, $\langle \hat{E}_r \hat{E}_s \rangle \neq 0$. Below we consider below two situations.

Case A. correspond to the generation of the coherent bi-photons along the axes of the pencil shape system of an inverted atomic system relative a dipole forbidden transition [19] together with two dipole active subsystems of radiators, S and R (see Ref. [23]). Here we propose another effect, in which the two-quantum cooperative emissions are ignited by single-photon decay process. As one-photon decay process of an exciting ensemble of atoms passes into Dicke super-fluorescence [24], we propose the situation in which this effect can be inhibited and the new cooperative interaction of this ensemble with dipole forbidden transitions of other atomic subsystems will stimulate another cooperative decay process, in which the coherence is established between the photon pairs. Indeed, if we consider an ensemble of excited atoms with non-equidistant transition energy, we may observe that in this situation the phase correlations between the atoms may be neglected. The non-equidistant dipole-active ensemble may be divided into two sub-ensembles of excited atoms, so that the pair of excited radiators from each sub-ensemble enters in resonance dipole-forbidden transition $(n + 1)S - nS$ of D of sub-ensemble D. In other words, we are interested in cooperative interaction between two dipole-active sub-ensembles and dipole-forbidden one as this is represented in **Figure 1**. Such super-radiance has the coherence between the photon-pairs and the coherence between the individual photons (first-order coherence) becomes inhibited.

Let us first discuss the three particle cooperative effects represented in **Figure 1** described in Refs. [17–19]. This interaction is focused on a new type of three particle collective spontaneous emission, in which the decay rate of three atomic subsystems is proportional to the product of the numbers of atoms in each subsystem, $N_s N_r N_d$ in the case all three sub-ensemble are equidistant. The quantum master equations take into consideration the correlations between three subsystems S, R and D in the single and two-photons cooperative exchanges between the atoms of each

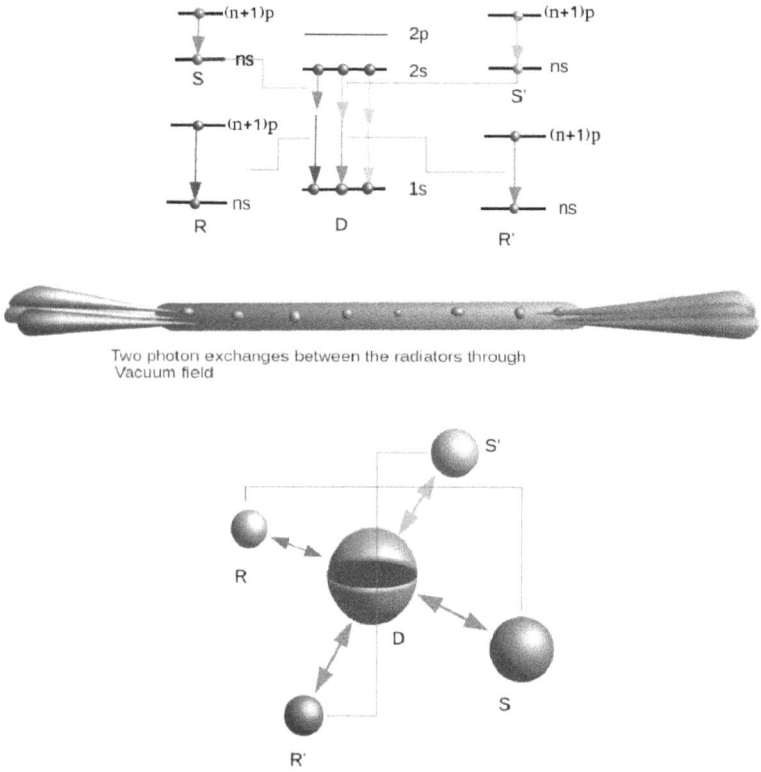

Figure 1.
The stimulation of two-photon cooperative effects of hydrogen-like (or helium-like) atomic transition $1S - 2S$ of D ensemble by dipole-active emission of S_j and R_j sub-ensembles in two-photon resonance described by the correlations (1a) and (1b). This two-photon cooperative decay can be prepared in pencil shape extended system of S, R and D radiators [19].

sub-ensemble (see Refs. [17–19]). The three-particles cooperative interaction through the vacuum of EMF is established taking into consideration the mutual influences between the single-photon polarization of S and R atomic subsystems and the non-linear polarization of the D atom (see Refs. [17–19]). To understand this effect it is necessary to examine the new correlation function which appears between the polarization of three different radiators from S, R and D subsystems: $\langle \hat{D}_n(t)\hat{R}_j^-(t)\hat{S}_l^-(t)\rangle$ and $\langle \hat{R}_l(t)\hat{S}_j(t)\hat{D}_m^-(t)\rangle$. The ignition role of S and R atoms is observed in the third-order terms, which contain two-photon resonances between three-particles represented in **Figure 1**, described by the above correlation functions. In order to experimentally observe these correlations, we must maximally destroy the single photon Dicke superradiance between atoms of S and R subsystems. This is possible if we choose the broadband sub-ensemble of excited dipole active atoms S and R. In this case, the single photon correlations between the atoms of this type become oscillatory with detuning frequency $\omega_{jl}^s(r)$ for j and l atoms. This corresponds to the situation when the correlations like $\langle \hat{S}_j(t)\hat{S}_l^-(t)\rangle$ (or $\langle \hat{R}_j(t)\hat{R}_l^-(t)\rangle$) become proportional to a $\exp[i\omega_{jl}^s(r)t]$ and rapidly oscillates during the cooperative decay process. But in this case in the sub-ensemble S, R we must have the big number of pairs $S_j, R_j, j = 1, 2, ..., N_p$ so that the established phase of each pair $\hat{S}_j^+$ and $\hat{R}_j^+$ will compensate the phase of $D_n^-(t)$ atom from equidistant D ensemble so that above defined three-particle correlators becomes smooth functions, giving the maximal contribution in two-photon decay of the ensemble. But in this case, the sums of the three-particle correlators on the indexes: j, l and m, containing non-equidistant two-level atoms, S, and R, becomes proportional to the number of pairs of this type of atoms and number of D atoms, $N_p N_d$.

In this situation is respect all resonance conditions between the pairs and equidistant D- ensemble: $2\omega_0 = \omega_{r_j} + \omega_{s_l}$. This resonance between the two-photon transitions of D atomic subsystem and the pairs of the two dipole active atoms of R and S subsystems is represented in **Figure 1**. We can extend our attention to a big ensemble of three particles in such a cooperative process. Three atoms D, R and S are situated at relative small distances r_{ds}, r_{dr} and r_{rs} in comparison with emission wavelength. Such atomic may file up the volume with a dimension larger than the emission wavelengths. The exchange energies between the subsystems were analyzed in the literature and an attractive problem is connected with pencil shape atomic mixture described above. In this situation, the radiation can be observed along the pencil-shape atomic system (see **Figure 1**).

Following this conception, we observe that for the big ensemble of radiators the first order correlation function $G_I(t, t+\tau) = \langle \hat{E}^{(-)}(t)\hat{E}^{(+)}(t+\tau) \rangle$ becomes smaller than second order one. The second order correlation functions between the photons can be divided into two parts: $G_{II}^b(t, t+\tau) = \langle \hat{E}^{(-)}(t)\hat{E}^{(-)}(t)\hat{E}^{(+)}(t+\tau)\hat{E}^{(+)}(t+\tau) \rangle$ and $G_{II}^s(t, t+\tau) = \langle \hat{E}^{(+)}(t)\hat{E}^{(-)}(t)\hat{E}^{(+)}(t+\tau)\hat{E}^{(-)}(t+\tau) \rangle$. The first part describes the correlation between the photon pairs generated into the broadband interval and the second part describes the correlation between the bi-modes of scattered field. Here the positive and negative parts of the field strength $\hat{E}^{(+)}(t) = \sum_k g_k \hat{a}_k(t) \exp[i(\mathbf{k}, \mathbf{r})]$ and $\hat{E}^{(-)}(t) = \sum_k g_k \hat{a}_k^\dagger(t) \exp[-i(\mathbf{k}, \mathbf{r})]$ are expressed through the superposition of the annihilation $\hat{a}_k(t)$ and generation $\hat{a}_k^\dagger(t)$ field operators with wave vector k and polarization λ respectively. Using the method of elimination operator developed in Ref. [19], we demonstrated, that the second order correlation function $G_{II}^b(t, t+\tau)$ between the bi-photons is proportional not only to the correlation function between the atoms of ensemble D but consists from the sum of two types of correlations, which contain the intrinsic correlation of D ensemble like in the Dicke process [24] and correlations between the D ensemble and dipole active sub-ensemble R and S $G_{II}^b(t, t+\tau) = G_{II}^{bi}(t, t+\tau) + G_{II}^{b(sr)}(t, t+\tau)$ according to the Refs. [17, 18] the correlation between the atoms of D ensemble is proportional to the function

$$G_{II}^{b(rs)}(t, t+\tau) \sim \int_0^{k_0} dk(k-k_0)^2 k^2 \sum_{j,n} \frac{\sin kr_{jn}}{kr_{jn}} \frac{\sin(k_0-k)r_{jn}}{(k_0-k)r_{jn}} \quad (1a)$$

$$\times \left\langle \hat{D}_j^+(t)\hat{D}_n^-(t+\tau) \right\rangle,$$

and two photon cooperative ignition by the S ad R subensamble

$$G_{II}^{b(rs)}(t, t+\tau) \sim \left\langle \hat{R}_l^+(t)\hat{S}_j^+(t)\hat{D}_n^-(t+\tau) \right\rangle \quad (1b)$$

$$\times \exp[i(\mathbf{k}_1 + \mathbf{k}, \mathbf{r}_n)] \exp[-i(\mathbf{k}', \mathbf{r}_j)] \exp[-i(\mathbf{k}', \mathbf{r}_l)].$$

Here we consider the sums on the repeated indexes. It is observed, that such a sum is proportional to the number dipole-active pairs N_p and number of D radiators. In the degenerate case when all three sub-ensemble are equidistant the number of term increase in the system [19], but in the system substantially increase first order coherence between the same photons. In other words, the single photon process substantially ignites the generation of coherent photon pairs.

In the second order of interaction of light with matter, these processes strongly connect two waves in the output detection schemes and they give us the possibility to distinguish the coherent effects between entangled photons. For traditional single-mode coherence, it is well known the possible lithographic limits in measurements $\Delta \geq \lambda/2$. Taking into account the concept about the dropped lithographic limit in two-quantum coherent processes, the authors of Ref. [20] proposed new lithographic limit in the two-photon processes with a magnitude two times smaller than traditional $\Delta \geq \lambda/4$. This take place when frequencies of the signal and idler photons have the same value $\omega_s = \omega_i$. This propriety is also contained and in two-photon super-radiance [21] but here $\lambda = 2\lambda_{si}\lambda_{ri}/(\lambda_{si} + \lambda_{ri})$. Here λ_{ri} and λ_{si} are the emitted wavelengths by S ad R from the pair i, $i = 1, 2, ..N_p$. An interesting effect of two photon cooperative emission is possible in micro-cavities. In this case the mode structure of the cavity stimulates the two-photon decay effect in comparison with cascade effect [19, 25, 26] (see **Figure 2**).

The coherent properties and entanglement between the photons, emitted in two-quantum lasers and parametric down conversion has a great impact on application in quantum information and communication. The possibility of induced two-photon generation per atomic transition was suggested by Sorokin, Braslau and Prohorov [27, 28]. The scattering effects in two-photon amplifier attenuate the possibility to realize two-photon lasing. The first experiments demonstrated that two-photon amplification and lasing in the presence of external sources are possible [16, 29]. These ideas open the new conception about the coherence. Indeed, introducing the amplitude of two-quantum field encapsulated in two-photon lasers we can observe that the generation amplitude is described by the field product

$$\hat{P}^{(+)}(t,z) = \hat{E}_s^+(z,t)\hat{E}_r^+(z,t)$$
$$= G(k_s, k_r)\hat{a}_s\hat{a}_r \exp\left[2i\omega_0 t - i(k_s + k_r)z\right], \qquad (2)$$

where $2\omega_0 = \omega_s + \omega_r = \omega_{21}$ is the total frequency of generated photons, $2k_0 = k_s + k_r$. In this case we can introduce the following operators of bi-boson field $\hat{I}^+ = \hat{a}_s^\dagger\hat{a}_r^\dagger$ and $\hat{I}^- = \hat{a}_s\hat{a}_r$; $\hat{I}_z = (\hat{a}_s^\dagger\hat{a}_s + \hat{a}_r^\dagger\hat{a}_r)/2$, which satisfy the commutation relations $[\hat{I}^+, \hat{I}^-] = -2\hat{I}_z$, $[\hat{I}_z, \hat{I}^\pm] = \pm\hat{I}^\pm$. Such a generation possibilities was proposed in Refs. [17, 18]. According to the representation of these operators, we may introduce the following coherent states for this field $|\mu\rangle = \exp(\mu\hat{I}^+)|j, j\rangle/1 - |\mu|^{2j}$, which belong to the $su(1, 1)$ symmetry described in Refs. [11, 19]. Here μ is the coherent displacement of bi-photon oscillator. Following this conception, the function $P^{(+)}(t, z)$ has the same behavior as the electrical component of single photon laser. For example, the mean value of this function on the coherent state can be represented through the harmonic functions with given phase and amplitude

$$\left\langle \hat{P}^{(+)}(t,z)\right\rangle = P_0 \exp\left[2i\omega_0 t - i(k_s + k_r)z + \varphi\right], \qquad (3)$$

where $P_0 = G(k_s, k_r)|\langle\hat{a}_s\hat{a}_r\rangle|$ is the amplitude and $\varphi = Arg\langle\hat{a}_s\hat{a}_r\rangle$ is the phase of electrical field strengths of two fields a and b. In the detection scheme represented in **Figure 2B** it is observe delay time through z-dependence of such functions. The lithographic limit follows from the difference between the maximum and minimum of two sit experiment represented in **Figure 2**. According to the expression (3) and the distinguish distance Δ between the slits follows, that the second

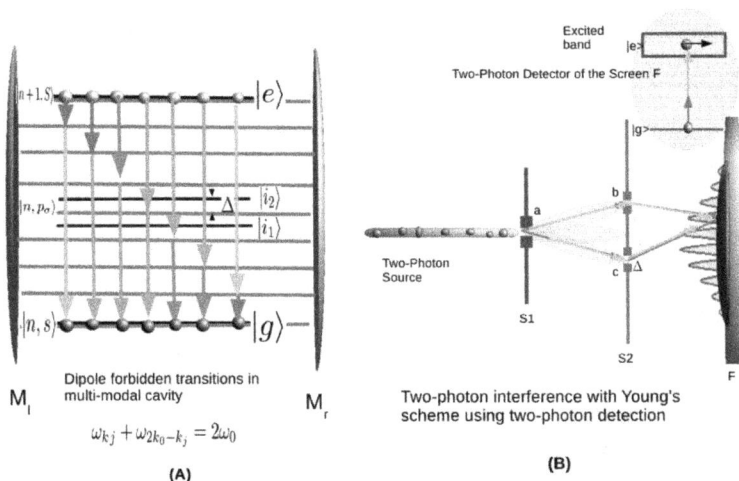

Figure 2.
(A) Sources of entangled photons in the two-photon bimodal processes. The horizontal blue lines represent the modes of the optical cavity modes formed between the vertical mirrors, M_l and M_r. (B) Two slits experiments with interference between pairs of modes which form the strengths product of EMF. The interference picture can be observed in tow-photon.

order correlation function $G_2(\Delta) = \langle \hat{P}^-(z)\hat{P}^+(z+\Delta) \rangle$ pass from maximal to minimal values for $\Delta(k_s + k_r)\sin\theta = \pi$. From this expression follows the some lithographic limit as in the Ref. [20].

To decorrelate the coherence between the photons of the same mode, in Ref. [10, 11] we proposed the cooperative multi-mode operators with similar commutation relations in the cavities. Mediating the amplitude of the bimodal fields we can introduce the collective modes field operators $\hat{I}^+ = \sum_{k \in (\omega_0, 0)} \hat{a}^\dagger_{2k_0-k}\hat{a}^\dagger_k$; $\hat{I}^- = \sum_{k \in (\omega_0, 0)} \hat{a}_{2k_0-k}\hat{a}_k$ and $\hat{I}_z = \sum_{k \in (\omega_0, 0)} (\hat{a}^\dagger_k\hat{a}_k + \hat{a}_{2k_0-k}\hat{a}^\dagger_{2k_0-k})/2$. As follows from above description the absolute value of conserved Casimir operator increase with increasing the number of bi-modes $\hat{I}^2 = (\hat{I}^z)^2 - 1/2(\hat{I}^+\hat{I}^- + \hat{I}^-\hat{I}^+)$. This effect is accompanied by the increasing of coherence between the bi-photons of each bi-modes relative the coherence which appears between the individual photons belonging to other modes. The similar coherent photon pairs may be generated in the broadband laser systems [11]. Following this idea the stationary solution of master equation for the bimodal cavity fled in the above multi-mode representation was obtained

$$\frac{\partial}{\partial t}\rho_m(t) = 2\kappa(m+1)(m+2j)\rho_{m+1}$$
$$-\frac{2(m+1)(m+2j)}{1+\beta(m+1)(m+2j)}\left(\alpha_1 + \alpha_2\frac{(m+1)(m+2j)}{1+\beta(m+1)(m+2j)}\right)\rho_m$$
$$+\alpha_2\frac{2m^2(m+2j-1)^2}{[1+\beta m(m+2j-1)]^2}\rho_{m-1} - Ibid\{m \to m-1\},$$

where $\alpha_1 = \frac{2|g|^2N\sigma_0\gamma}{(\omega-2\omega_0)^2+\gamma^2}$ represents the generation rate of photon pairs for full atomic inversion $N\sigma_0$, $\alpha_2 = \frac{T}{N\sigma_0}(\alpha_1^2 + \chi^2)$, $\beta = \frac{4|g|^2T\gamma}{(\omega-2\omega_0)^2+\gamma^2}$, and $\chi = \frac{2|g|^2N\sigma_0(\omega-2\omega_0)}{(\omega-2\omega_0)^2+\gamma^2}$. Here we used decomposition of density operator of bimodal field in the cavity $\rho(t) = \sum_{m=0}\rho_m|m,j\rangle\langle m,j|$. The evolution of correlation of the bi-photon intensity

$\langle \hat{I}^{+}(t)\hat{I}^{-}(t)\rangle$, and the sum of the photon correlation functions in each mode d $\langle : \hat{n}^{2} : \rangle$ to lasing phase transition point for the following values of the j—collective parameter: $j = 0.5$ and $j = 10$. Here $\hat{n} = 2(\hat{I}_{z} - j)$. It is observed that with the increase of the number of the bi-modes the coherence between the bimodal field characteristic $\hat{P}^{-}(t + \tau, z)$ and $\hat{P}^{+}(t, z)$ increases: $\rangle\hat{P}^{-}(t + \tau, z)\hat{P}^{+}(t, z)$ $\langle \hat{I}^{+}(t)\hat{I}^{-}(t)\rangle \exp[2i\omega_{0}\tau - 2ik_{0}z]$. As it is observed from the behavior of parameter $\langle : n^{2} : \rangle$, with increasing the number of modes, j, the coherence between the individual photons substantially decreases (see **Figure 3a** and **b**). This process of lasing stabilization is accompanied by the increasing the coherence between the photon pairs belonging to conjugate bi-modes and may be detected by the scheme represented in **Figure 2B**. The generation process of the coherent field in the some mode of the ensemble of the modes $2j$ is described by the sum of correlations $\sum_{k}\langle \hat{E}_{k}^{(-)}(t + \tau)\hat{E}_{k}^{(+)}(t)\rangle$, which become proportional to the sum of number of photons in each mode $\langle \hat{n}\rangle \exp[i\varphi(\tau)]$. As follows from **Figure 3** the amplitude of this function achieved the small all value with the increasing of the number of modes. In the single photon detection this correlations is described by the aleatory phase $\varphi(\tau)$ and may be represented by the smooth function (see "red" line) on the screen F of interference scheme **Figure 2B**.

Case B. Another possibility to create a coherent field for a big number of photons distributed in the broadband spectrum represents the bimodal spectrum of scattered photons. Indeed if we represent superposition between the photons obtained from A and S atoms as a combination $|\psi\rangle \sim |1\rangle_{a}|0\rangle_{s} + \exp i\phi|0\rangle_{a}|1\rangle_{s}/\sqrt{2}$ we may extrapolate such superposition for a big number of atoms from the dipole active sub-ensemble A and S belonging to $su(2)$ symmetry. Let us first discuss the three particle cooperative effects in the scattering interaction represented in **Figure 4** [17–19]. In the free space, such field may be generated with pencil shape process described by three ensembles of atoms D, S and A . This description is devoted to this a new type of three particle collective spontaneous emission, in which the decay rate of three atomic subsystems is proportional to the product of the numbers of atoms in each sub ensemble of equidistant atoms, $N_{s}N_{r}N_{d}$. In this situation only one possibility of resonance interaction between the dipole forbidden transition of D-Lambda atoms and ensemble of dipole active atoms S and A

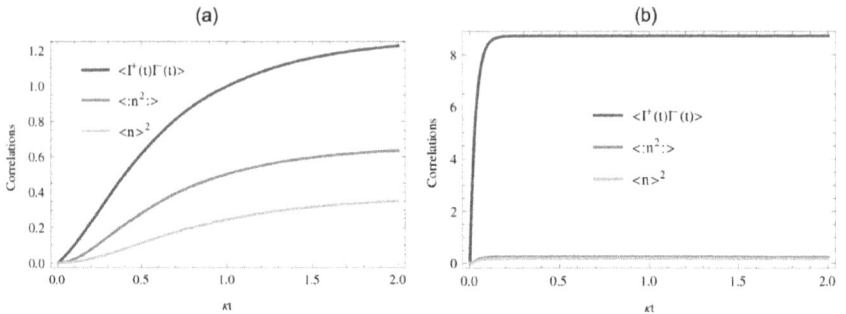

Figure 3.
The evolution of the photon correlations as function of the relative time $t\kappa$ to the phase transition for following parameters of the system: $\alpha_{1}/\kappa = 0.4$, $\alpha_{1}/\kappa = 0.01$ and $\beta/\kappa = 0.001$. Here it is represented: the square amplitudes of bimodal field $\langle \hat{I}^{+}\hat{I}^{-}\rangle$ (blue line), the correlation between the photons of each mode, $\langle : \hat{n}^{2} : \rangle$ (red line) and the square of mean value of the photon number in each mode, $\langle \hat{n}\rangle^{2}$ (green line). Figure a corresponds to single mode two-photon emission, $j = 1/2$, and the numerical representation in figure b corresponds to the number of the bimodal cavity field $2j = 20$. As follows for the figures a and b the total photon correlations in each mode decreases with the increasing of the number of bi-modes (see the red and green lines).

Two-quantum cooperative scattering with absorption and emission of photons between A, S and D subsystems

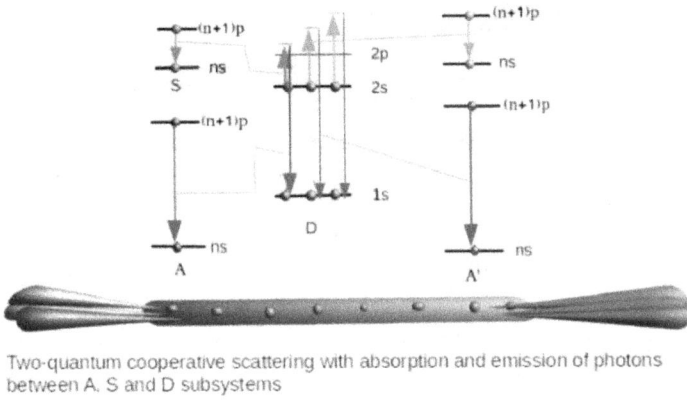

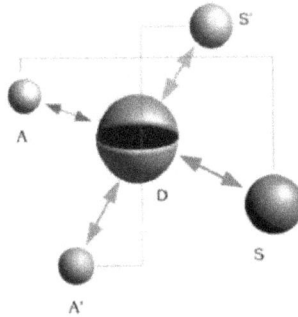

Figure 4.
The similar mutual transitions between dipole-active A_j and S_j atoms in scattering resonance with hydrogen-like (or helium like) ensemble of D atoms, described by the expression (4).

$2\omega_0 = \omega_a - \omega_s$, which correspond to scattering resonance between the three parti-cles, respectively. This resonance situation for the decorrelated ensemble of dipole active atoms is represented in **Figure 4**.

We observe, that the Dicke cooperative effects between the sub-ensemble of atoms, S, and A can be neglected if the atoms in the sub-ensembles S and A are not equidistant relative their excited energy. In such a situation the Dicke cooperative effect in sub-systems of dipole-active atoms is negligible due to the consideration that the frequency width of broadband emission $\Delta\omega$ is large than the cooperative emission rate Γ_c. In this situation the cooperative correlations like $\langle \hat{A}_j^+(t)\hat{A}_l^-(t)\rangle$ and $\langle \hat{S}_j^+(t)\hat{S}_l^-(t)\rangle$ become proportional to the rapid oscillatory parts $\exp\left[i(\omega_{aj} - \omega_{al})t\right]$ and $\exp\left[i(\omega_{sj} - \omega_{sl})t\right]$, and vanishes after an average procedure on the time interval less than the decay time $1/\Gamma_c$. In such a situation, only the pairs of S, and A sub ensembles can excite the D-subsystem according to the third-order of perturbation decomposition [19]. It contains three particle scattering exchanges between the pairs of S, and A atoms and D-an ensemble of equidistant atomic represented by **Figure 4**. This exchange scheme of two S and A atomic pairs is described by the correlations between the pairs of A and S scattering resonance with D:
$\langle \hat{S}_j^+(t)\hat{D}_m^+(t)\hat{A}_l^-(t)\rangle$, $\langle \hat{A}_j^+(t)\hat{S}_l^-(t)\hat{D}_m^-(t)\rangle$ described by master equation in Ref. [23]. It corresponds to the scattering resonance between the pairs and D ensemble:
$\omega_{aj} - \omega_{sj} - 2\omega_0 = 0$. Here $i = 1, 2, N_p$, N_d is the number of atomic pairs of S and A sub-ensembles. In this situation, the second order coherence is also proportional to the product of two superposition of D-atoms and pairs of S_i and A_i atoms in the scattering resonance with D-equidistant ensemble as in the two-photon resonance

$$G_{II}^s(t, t+\tau) \sim \left\langle \hat{A}_l^+(t)\hat{S}_j^-(t+\tau)\hat{D}_n^-(t+\tau) \right\rangle$$

$$\times \exp\left[i(\mathbf{k}_1 + \mathbf{k}, \mathbf{r}_n)\right] \exp\left[-i(\mathbf{k}', \mathbf{r}_j)\right] \exp\left[-i(\mathbf{k}', \mathbf{r}_l)\right]. \tag{4}$$

As follows from the expression (4) and the scattering generation of correlation photons in the cavity **Figure 4** the scattered field into the blocs of two-modes ω_{ai}; ω_{si} and ω_{al}; ω_{sl} can form the coherent $su(2)$ state, which corresponds to the generators of the superposition of collective discrete bi-modes of EMF $\hat{J}^- = \sum_k \hat{a}_k^\dagger \hat{a}_{k+2k_0}$, $\hat{J}^+ = \sum_k \hat{a}_{k+2k_0}^\dagger \hat{a}_k$ and $\hat{J}_z = \sum_k \{\hat{a}_{k+2k_0}^\dagger \hat{a}_{k+2k_0} - \hat{a}_k^\dagger \hat{a}_k\}/2$ which satisfies the commutation relations for $su(2)$ algebra described in Section 2. In this cooperative effect, due to large number non-equidistant atoms in each ensemble A or S, the frequency differences between the scattered modes $\omega_{ai} - \omega_{si} = 2\omega_0$ and $\omega_{al} - \omega_{sl}$ have same wave vectors, $K_i = K_l$, where $\mathbf{K}_i = \mathbf{k}_{ai} - \mathbf{k}_{si}$ and $\mathbf{K}_l = \mathbf{k}_{al} - \mathbf{k}_{sl}$ and can be used in the coherent phenomena like holograms, or optical processing. In such coherence it is manifested the correlations between the ensemble of bi-modes generated by the pairs of atoms $\{S_l, A_l\}$, $l = 1, ...N_p$. These effects are accompanied with the interference between single- and two-quantum collective transitions of three inverted radiators from the ensemble. The three particle collective decay rate is defined in the description of the atomic correlation functions.

Let us study the interaction between the molecular systems and external Raman field prepared in the cooperative coherent process proposed in Refs. [12, 13, 30]. Following this Refs [19, 23], we can introduced the bimodal operators the product of which oscillates with the frequency $2\omega_0$ near the vibration frequency of the molecules (or bio-molecules) Ω

$$\hat{\Pi}^{(-)}(t,z) = \lambda\hat{E}_p^{(+)}(z,t)\hat{E}_a^{(-)}(z,t) + g\hat{E}_s^{(+)}(z,t)\hat{E}_p^{(-)}(z,t)$$

$$= G(k_p, k_a)\hat{b}\hat{a}^\dagger \exp\left[2i\omega_0 t - i(k_a - k_p)z\right] \tag{5}$$

$$+ G(k_s, k_p)\hat{s}\hat{b}^\dagger \exp\left[2i\omega_0 t - i(k_p - k_s)z\right].$$

Here the annihilation (creation) operators, $\hat{b}(\hat{b}^\dagger)$, $\hat{s}(\hat{s}^\dagger)$ and $\hat{a}(\hat{a}^\dagger)$, correspond to the pump, Stokes and anti-Stokes modes, respectively, which satisfy the Bose commutation rules: $[\hat{a}_i, \hat{a}_j^\dagger] = \delta_{j,i}$, and $[\hat{a}_i, \hat{a}_j] = 0, j \equiv a, b, s)$. The interaction Hamiltonian of molecules (bio-molecules) with bimodal field is described by the Hamiltonian $\hat{H}_I = -\hat{P}(t,z)\hat{\Pi}^-(t,z) + H.c.$, where the vector $\hat{P}$ is proportional to the displacement of the molecular oscillator $\hat{P}(t,z) \sim \hat{Q}(t,z) \sim |e\rangle\langle g| + |g\rangle\langle e|$. In the interaction with atomic sub-system (for example, four level system represented in **Figure 5**) in many situations $\lambda \sim \hbar/\Delta_a$ and $g \sim \hbar/\Delta_s$. From commutation of the bi-photon field operators between them $[g\hat{s}\hat{b}^\dagger + \lambda\hat{b}\hat{a}^\dagger, g\hat{b}\hat{s}^\dagger + \lambda\hat{a}\hat{b}^\dagger] = g^2(\hat{b}^\dagger\hat{b} - \hat{s}\hat{s}^\dagger + 1) + \lambda^2(\hat{a}^\dagger\hat{a} - \hat{b}\hat{b}^\dagger + 1)$, it is not difficult to observe that, when the interaction constant of atoms with Stokes and anti-Stokes modes coincide $g = \lambda$, the new operators, belonging to angular momentum $SU(2)$ symmetry, can be easily introduced: $\hat{L}_z = \hat{a}^\dagger\hat{a} - \hat{s}^\dagger\hat{s}$, $\hat{L}^- = \sqrt{2}(\hat{b}\hat{s}^\dagger + \hat{a}\hat{b}^\dagger)$, $\hat{L}^+ = \sqrt{2}(\hat{s}\hat{b}^\dagger + \hat{b}\hat{a}^\dagger)$. The similar commutation relation can be obtained in the case, when the relations $\lambda \gg g$ or $\lambda \ll g$ are satisfied. In the last two cases we may neglect the Stokes or anti-Stokes scattering process so, that the similar operators may be defined for this two special situations: (a) $\hat{J}^- = \hat{a}\hat{b}^\dagger; \hat{J}^+ = \hat{b}\hat{a}^\dagger$, $\hat{J}_z = (\hat{a}^\dagger\hat{a} - \hat{b}^\dagger\hat{b})/2$ for $\lambda \gg g$ and (b) $\hat{J}^- = \hat{b}\hat{s}^\dagger$, $\hat{J}^+ = \hat{s}\hat{b}^\dagger, \hat{J}_z = (\hat{b}^\dagger\hat{b} - \hat{s}^\dagger\hat{s})/2$ for $\lambda \ll g$. The commutation relations between these

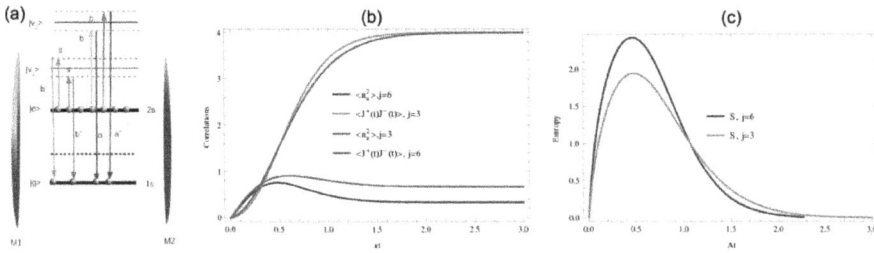

Figure 5.
*(a) The Raman excitation of radiators (atoms, molecules) in the four-level energetic scheme with the conversion of the photons in stokes and anti-Stokes modes. Such atoms may fling through the cavity in **Figure 2A**. (b) The time evolution of the relative correlations $\langle \hat{J}^-(t)\hat{J}^-(t)\rangle/j^2$ and $\langle n^2\rangle/j^2$ for following parameters of the system $\beta/A = 0.015$, $j = 3$ and $j = 6$. (c) Evolution of von Neumann entropy for some parameters of the system. The substantial increase of the coherence between the bi-modal fields in comparison with coherence between the total numbers of photons belonging to each mode is observed. The entropy achieved minimal value in the lasing phase with increasing the number of uncorrelated modes in the pump and anti-Stokes field.*

operators are similar to the commutators of the collective atomic operators:
$[\hat{L}^+, \hat{L}^-] = 2\hat{L}_z$ and $[\hat{L}_z, \hat{L}^\pm] = \pm\hat{L}^\pm$. According to this description the new interaction Hamiltonian, $\hat{H}_I = \frac{\hbar g}{\sqrt{2}}\{|g\rangle\langle e|\hat{L}^\dagger + |e\rangle\langle g|\hat{L}^-\}$. Using the decomposition on the small operator of the system, $\hat{x}/(1+\hat{x})$, we may estimate the quantum fluctuations and the correlation functions as a function of evolution time and photon number in the applied field. Here $\hat{x} = 2\varepsilon\hat{L}^-\hat{L}^\dagger$ proportional to the small parameter $\varepsilon = g^2\gamma^{-2}$ described in Refs. [12, 31] ($\gamma^{-1} = \Lambda/v$ is main value of the flying time of atom, expressed through the atomic velocity, v, and cavity length, Λ). According to the projection operator method developed in Ref. [31] we start from the first order approximation of the master equation

$$\frac{d}{dt}\hat{W}(t) = -A\left[\hat{W}(t)\hat{L}^-\frac{1}{1+2\varepsilon\hat{L}^-\hat{L}^\dagger},\hat{L}^\dagger\right] + H.c.,$$

where $A = Ng^2/2$ is the conversion rate, $\beta = 2A\varepsilon$ is the attenuation of the conversion rate, which increases with the increasing the mean value of the lifetime of the excited N-atoms flings through the cavity. The numerical solution of this equation is obtained, decomposing the density matrix on the angular momentum states, described by the eigenstates of the operator $\hat{L}^2$, $\hat{W} = \sum_{m=-j}^{j} P_m(t)|j, m\rangle\langle m, j|$. Here the Hilbert vectors $|j, m\rangle$ belong to the three mode states in the resonator (Pump, Stokes and anti-Stokes), $P_m(t)$ is the population probability of the $|j, m\rangle$ state. As in the two-photon emission (Case A) we are interested in the developing of the quantum between the photons belonging to scattered bi-modes. As a simple representation, we consider the situation when the non-correlated photons from the pump mode "b" is converted into the anti-Stokes mode "b". This process is possible for big detuning from resonance $\Delta_1 \gg \Delta_2$ (see **Figure 5a**). As follows from the interaction Hamiltonian in this situation the coherent function $G_2(\tau) = \langle \hat{\Pi}^-(t, z)\hat{\Pi}^+(t + \tau, z)\rangle$ becomes proportional to the expression $\langle \hat{J}^-(t)\hat{J}^-(t)\rangle \exp[i2\omega_0\tau]$. From **Figure 5** follows that in the process of conversion of the un-correlated pump photons into the anti-Stokes one $n_a = j + \langle \hat{J}_z(t)\rangle$ the cooperative phase of these two modes is established. The process achieved the saturation phase like in the single photon lasers. With the increasing the number of uncorrelated pump photons in broadband of the modes, this process is accompanied with the decreasing of relative coherence of the photons in each mode, so that the sum of total converted photons in anti-Stokes modes remain smaller than second order coherent function $G_2(0)$

(see **Figure 5**). The von Neumann entropy of the system, obtained from the representation $S_t = \sum_{m=-j}^{j} P_m \log [P_m]$ achieves the maximal value at the initial stage of conversion after that when it is established the coherence between the pump photons and converted one like in a similar way like in the super-radiance. After that, it decreases correspond to the established a new coherent phase described above.

Let us find the coherent phenomena which appears between two fields in Raman processes. If we study generation of Stokes light under the non-coherent pumping with anti-Stokes field, we can introduce the following representation of the bi-modal field

$$\hat{\Pi}^-(t,z) = \hat{E}_s^{(+)}(z,t)\hat{E}_a^-(z,t) = G(k_s, k_a)\hat{a}\hat{b}^\dagger \exp[2i\omega_0 t - i(k_a - k_s)z], \qquad (6)$$

where $\hat{E}_s^{(+)}(z,t)$ and $\hat{E}_a^-(z,t)$ are positive and negative defined strength of Stokes and anti-Stokes field (see **Figure 5a**), $\hat{a}_s^\dagger, \hat{b}_a^\dagger$ and $\hat{a}_s, \hat{b}_a$ are the annihilation and creation operators of electromagnetic field at Stokes, ω_s, and anti-Stokes, ω_a, frequencies respectively; $\omega_a - \omega_s = \omega_0$ is the fixed frequency of bi-modal field according to transition diagram represented in **Figure 5**. Following this definition one can introduced the new bi-quantum operators $\hat{J}^- = \hat{b}^\dagger\hat{a}; \hat{J}^+ = \hat{a}^\dagger\hat{b}$; and $\hat{J}_z = (\hat{a}^+\hat{a} - \hat{b}^\dagger\hat{b})/2$. In this case for constant number of photons in resonator the conservation of Kasimir vector is possible, $\hat{J}^2 = \hat{J}_z^2 + \hat{J}_x^2 + \hat{J}_y^2$, where $\hat{J}_x = (\hat{J}^+ + \hat{J}^-)/2, \hat{J}_y = (\hat{J}^+ - \hat{J}^-)/2i$. Considering that initially the photons are prepared in anti-Stokes mode of cavity $N = 2j$, one can describe the two photon scattering lasing processes by coherent state for this bi-boson field, belonging to $su(2)$ algebra.

$$|\alpha\rangle = \exp\left\{\alpha\hat{J}^+\right\}|-j,j\rangle\left\{1 + |\alpha|^2\right\}^{-j}, \qquad (7)$$

where $\alpha = \tan(\theta/2)$ is the amplitude of this bi-boson field obtained in the Raman lasing processes. Taking into account the coherent state (7) one can found the mean value of strength product $\langle\hat{\Pi}(t,z)\rangle = [\langle\hat{\Pi}^-(t,z)\rangle + \langle\hat{\Pi}^+(t,z)\rangle]/2$

$$\langle\hat{\Pi}(t,z)\rangle = \Pi_0 \cos[\omega_0 t - (k_a - k_s)z + \varphi], \qquad (8)$$

where $\Pi_0 = G(k_s, k_a)|\langle\hat{a}_s\hat{b}_a^+\rangle|$ and $\varphi = \arg\langle\hat{a}_s\hat{b}_a^+\rangle$ are the amplitude and phase of bimodal field formed from Stokes and anti-Stokes photons.

The lithographic limit between maximal and minimal values of amplitude of correlation function $G_2(\Delta) = \langle\Pi^-(z)\Pi^+(z + \Delta)\rangle$ in the two-slit experiments observed with two-photon detectors corresponds to the lithographic limit of this conjugate entangled bimodal field (see **Figure 6**). In this case, this limit is larger than in two-photon coherent emission $\Delta \geq \lambda_p\lambda_s/[2(\lambda_s - \lambda_p)]$. The frequency of this coherent field achieves the frequency of the vibration states of the molecule (bio-molecules) when the difference of wavelengths between the Stokes, pump, and anti-Stokes have the same magnitude. This coherent phenomenon between the Stokes and anti-Stokes fields can be used in Holographic representation of molecular vibrations and other coherent processes with phase memory. For holography, we propose the generation of new coherent states between Stokes pump and anti-Stokes field using nano-fiber systems [32]. In comparison with the cavity field, this type of generation permits to use the correlated bi modes out-site of generation

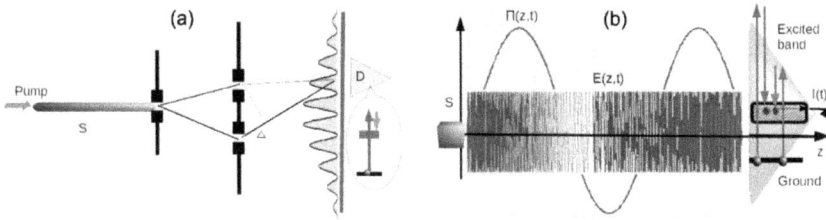

Figure 6.
*(a) The non-coherent pump of the bimodal field in the cavity (see **Figure 5a**) and scattering double slit interference on the frequency, $2\omega_0 = \omega_p - \omega_s$. (b) The time dependence of the mean value of vector $\langle \hat{\Pi}(z,t) \rangle$ (black line) and phase aliasing distribution in Raman components of the field $E(z,t)$. For the detection of the coherent properties (6)-(8) of $\langle \hat{\Pi}(z,t) \rangle$, it is possible to use a two-photon detection scheme.*

scheme represented in **Figure 9**. The atoms situated in the evanescent zone of nano-fiber stimulate the cooperative conversion of the photons from anti-Stokes pulse into the pump and Stokes pulses.

3. Quantum communication and holographic proprieties of bi-boson coherent field

The main differences between this bimodal field and the classical coherent field consists in the aleatory distribution of energies and phases between the photons of each pair, which enter in the coherent ensemble of bi-photons. Passing through the dispersion media's the common phrase of the ensemble may be drastically destroyed so, that the problem which appear consist in the restoration of common phase of the ensemble of photon pairs generated by the quantum sources. These phenomena of restoration of common phase of the ensemble have a quantum aspects and can be used in quantum communication and quantum holography.

In the case A we proposed the new possibilities in decreasing of coherent proprieties between the photon pairs of two-photon beam. The application of coherent effect of the bimodal field of communication and holography opens the new perspectives in the transmission of information not only through entangled state of photons but also through the second order coherence. At the first glance one observes that such coherent registration of information may have nothing to do with the traditional method. But looking to the scheme of **Figure 7** we observe that when the photon-pair pulses pass through a dispersive medium, the idler photons from the pair change their directions relative to signal photons. Focusing the signal and idler photons into different optical fibers, we are totally dropping the coherence among the photons. However, after a certain time interval, the idler and signal photons from the pairs could be mixed again (see **Figure 7**) and the coherence may be restored. The coherent state obtained in two-photon cooperative or laser emission takes into account not only entanglement between the pairs of photons, but the coherence between the bi-photons too, and can be used in mixed processing problems in which the quantum entanglement between the photon of each pair of photons is used simultaneously with classical coherence between the pairs.

Below we discuss how hologram can be constructed using the recording phase information of bimodal field on a medium sensitive to this phase, using two separate beams of bimodal field (one is the "usual" beam associated with the image to be recorded and the other is a known as the reference beam). Exploiting the interference pattern between these bi-boson fields described in the last section in principle this is possible. For example the Stokes and anti-Stokes fields can be regarded as a field with electromagnetic strength product (6), so that the common phases $\phi = 2\omega_0 t - k_0 z$ of

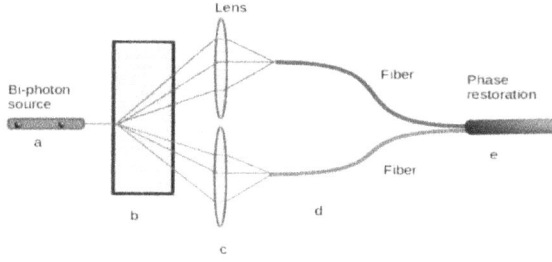

Figure 7.
The two-quanta coherence and its possible experimental observations: a, two photon coherent generator; b, dispersive media; c, lenses; d, fibers; e, signal restoration.

these two fields amplitude a_s and b_a^+ has similar behavior as the phase of single mode coherent field, here $2\omega_0 = \omega_a - \omega_s$ and $k_0 = k_a - k_s$ are the frequencies and wave vector difference between the Stokes and anti-Stokes fields respectively. The coherent propriety of this product of the electric field components is proposed to apply in possibilities to construct the time, space holograms of real objects, taking in to account the conservation of phase of amplitude product in the propagating and interference processes. The quantum phase between the radiators can also be used in holography.

Presently exist a lot of proposals in which is manifested holographic principals of processing of quantum information [5, 8, 9]. One of them is the model of Prof. Teich with co-authors [5]. According to this model the correlations between the entangled photons, obtained in parametric down conversion, can be used in quantum holography. The hologram in parametrical down conversion is realized in terms of the correlations between the entangled photon in the single pair. The coherence between the pairs is not taken into consideration.

Following the idea of classical holograms, we changed the conception of two-photon holograms using the second order interference described in Refs. [19, 30]. This new type of hologram registration is based on the coherent proprieties (3) and (8). As well known the holographic code in single photon coherent effects appears on mixing the original wave (hereafter called the "object wave") I_0 with a known "reference wave" I_r and recording their interference pattern in the $z = 0$ plane. According to transmittance conception T of single-mode holograms, the correlations are proposed in the strength product of "object wave" and the "reference wave" waves $\langle \hat{E}_O(z,t)\hat{E}_r(z,t+\tau)\rangle$, where $\hat{E}_O(z,t) = (\hat{E}_O^+(z,t) + \hat{E}_O^-(z,t))/\sqrt{2}$ and $\hat{E}_r(z,t+\tau) = (\hat{E}_r^+(z,t+\tau) + \hat{E}_r^-(z,t+\tau))/\sqrt{2}$ the scheme of interference pattern is represented in **Figure 8** and has many analogies with classical holograms. The transmittance is given by interference between the original and reference bimodal waves at t (see for example [33]). Extending this conception we construct such a hologram, replacing the EMF strength the two-photon coherence using the field vector (2)-(3). According to the classical definition one can represent correlations between the original bimodal field through $\hat{P}_O(z,t) = (\hat{P}_O^+(z,t) + \hat{P}_O^-(z,t))/\sqrt{2}$ and reference bimodal wave vector, described by the expression $\hat{P}_r(z,t+\tau) = (\hat{P}_r^+(z,t+\tau) + \hat{P}_r^-(z,t+\tau))/\sqrt{2}$. In this case, the points on the plan of hologram, $z = 0$, we have the transmittance

$$T_b = \left\langle : \left(\hat{P}_O(z,t) + \hat{P}_r(z,t+\tau)\right)^2 : \right\rangle$$

$$= \left\langle \hat{P}_O^-(0,t)\hat{P}_O^+(0,t)\right\rangle + \langle \hat{P}_r^-(0,t+\tau)(\hat{P}_r^+(0,t+\tau)\rangle \qquad (9)$$

$$+ \left\langle \hat{P}_O^-(0,t)\hat{P}_r^+(0,t+\tau)\right\rangle + \left\langle \hat{P}_r^-(0,t+\tau)\hat{P}_O^+(0,t)\right\rangle.$$

In the expression (9) the function $G_{O2} = \langle \hat{P}_O^-(0,t)\hat{P}_O^+(0,t)\rangle$ represents the intensity of detecting bi-photons from the original bimodal field; $G_{r2} = \langle \hat{P}_r^-(0,t+\tau)\hat{P}_r^+(0,t+\tau)\rangle$ is the intensity of detecting bi-photons from reference bimodal wave from the object. The phase dependence of the image can be described by argument of complex number $\langle P_O^-(0,t)P_r^+(0,t+\tau)\rangle$ or $\arg(\hat{P}_O^+(0,t)) - \arg(\hat{P}_r^+(r,t+\tau))$. The propriety of two-photon bimodal field is described by the expressions (2)–(3) of the last Section 2. The detection scheme on the plan $z = 0$ is described in **Figure 8** and as in the scheme 7, we may take into consideration the fact, that the coherent blocks of bi-photons can be separated into idler and signal photons. This entangled effect may be registered by two separate detector screens represented in the **Figure 8**. For example the A screen, it is used for the registration of 'idler' photons while the screen B can be used for the registration of amplitude an fluctuations phase of 'signal' photons. The problem consists in the restoration of this bimodal field with coherent proprieties between the bi-photons. The transmittance can be detected by two photon detectors on the plane (x,y) and the interpretation of image can be expressed in classical terms

$$T_b = G_{O2} + G_{r2} + 2\sqrt{G_{r2}G_{O2}} \cos\left[\arg(P_O^+(0,t)) - \arg(P_r^+(r,t+\tau))\right] \quad (10)$$

The same behavior has the bimodal field formed from Stokes Pump and anti-Stokes photons. In the case of scattering bimodal field the coherent proprieties of the vector $\Pi_O(z,t) = (\Pi_O^+(z,t) + \Pi_O^-(z,t))/\sqrt{2}$ can be found from the expressions (5)–(8) so that the transmittance

$$T_s = \left\langle : (\Pi_O(z,t) + \Pi_r(z,t+\tau))^2 : \right\rangle$$

$$= \langle \Pi_O^-(0,t)\Pi_O^+(0,t)\rangle + \langle \Pi_r^-(0,t+\tau)\Pi_r^+(0,t+\tau)\rangle \quad (11)$$

$$+ \langle \Pi_O^-(0,t)\Pi_r^+(0,t+\tau)\rangle + \langle \Pi_r^-(0,t+\tau)\Pi_O^+(0,t)\rangle.$$

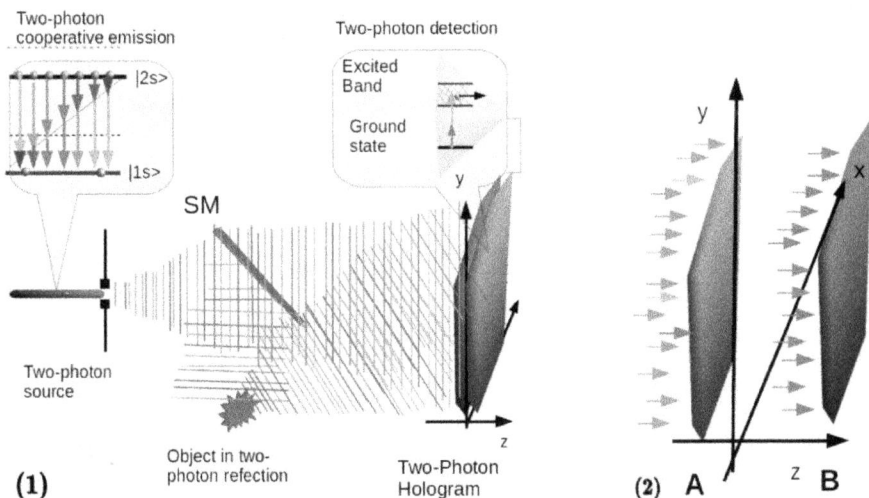

Figure 8.
(1) Two-photon coherent light described in Section 2 and the registration of hologram taking into consideration the phase and amplitude of bi-photon field of the "object" and "reference" waves. (2) The possibilities to detect the "signal" ($\omega_i \in (\omega_0, 2\omega_0)$) and "idler" ($\omega_i \in (0, \omega_0)$) photons on separate screens A and B.

This type of Holography takes into consideration the coherent process at low frequency $\omega_p - \omega_s$ (or $\omega_a - \omega_p$ which may coincide with the vibration frequencies of biomolecules. The popularity of coherent Raman scattering techniques in optical microscopy increases and it may be developed using another type of coherence described in the section. The holography developed on the bases of coherence proprieties between the two- (or three) conjugate modes of the scattering field opens this possibility not only for the description of the spectral diapason and time dependence of scattered field intensity, but the topological aspects of the molecular structures manifested in holographic representations of the vibrational modes of molecules. The coherence proposed in the Section 2 B needs the low intensity of each mode component in comparison with traditional Raman diagnostic proposed in Refs. [14, 15]. Using the coherent proprieties, described at the point B of the last section, we can estimate a lot of peculiarities connected with geometrical structures of biomolecules for lower intensities of each mode component of Raman process described by Refs. [14, 15]. In this case the transmission can be detected by the scheme proposed in **Figure 9** on the plan (x, y), where the interpretation of Hologram imaging can be expressed in classical terms.

$$T_s = G_{O2} + G_{r2} + 2\sqrt{G_{r2}G_{O2}}\cos\left[\arg\left(\Pi_O^+(0, t)\right) - \arg\left(\Pi_r^+(r, t + \tau)\right)\right] \quad (12)$$

The entanglement between each mode of the field can be detected by two-photon detector schemes, placed in the plan of hologram represented in **Figure 9**. This procedure may be in tangency with proposed experimental detections of vibration modes of biomolecules [8, 9].

In comparison with the spontaneous parametric down-conversion the super-radiance [21] or cooperative scattering processes [12, 13] represented generators of non-classical light source—the two-photon quantum entangled state with the coherent aspects between the two conjugate modes. Two-modes from such processes may become incoherent, but the coherence can be revived in the two-photon excitations of the detector which represents the photon pairs from adjacent modes. The two-photon detection scheme an interference connected to it is shown in **Figure 6**. The similar effect appears between stokes, pump, and anti-Stokes photon in induced scattering. In the pioneer theoretical work of two-photon optics, Belinskii and Klyshko [7] predicted three spooky schemes: two-photon diffraction, two-photon holography, and two-photon transformation of two-dimensional images. The first and last schemes have been demonstrated in the experiments,

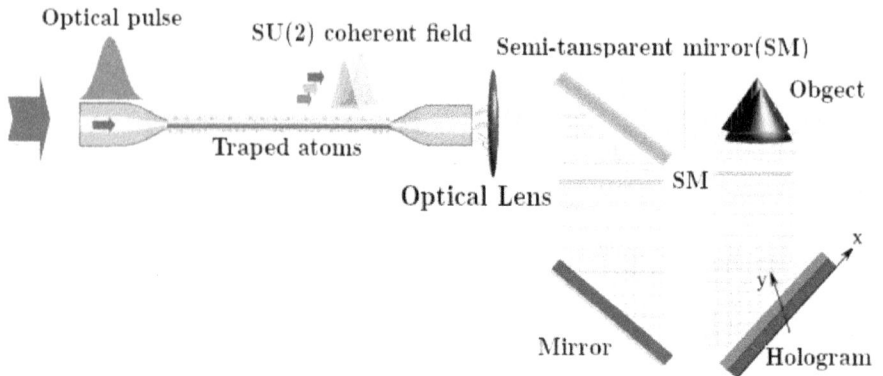

Figure 9.
Two-photon coherent light and principle of hologram registration taking into consideration the phase and amplitude of the three modes of Raman scattered field Stokes, pump and anti-Stokes modes.

known as ghost interference [34] and ghost imaging [35], respectively. These experiments are connected to the original gedankenexperiment of EPR paradox and open the way to the detection of two-photon holography [8, 9]. In such holograms the signal photons play both roles of "object wave" and "reference wave" in holography, but are recorded by a point detector providing only encoding information, while the "idler" photons travel freely and are locally manipulated with spatial resolution along the fibers becomes possible.

4. Conclusions

The encrypted information, using the coherence of multi-mode bimodal field in quantum holography, opens the new perspective, in which the coherence proprieties between bi-photons are used together with non-local states of entangled photon pairs. The possibilities to use this coherence in the quantum communication and holographic registration of objects is described by the expressions (9) and (10) and is proposed for future developments. The main distinguish between the traditional holograms and such a hologram registration becomes attractive from physical points of view because it must take into consideration the common phase of two light modes described by the expressions (9)-(12). It also discusses the cooperative behavior of three cavity modes which corresponds to pump, Stokes and anti-Stokes photons stimulated by the atomic inversion. A new type of cooperative generation described by the correlations of the expressions (1) and (4) may be used in quantum nucleonics [36] as an ignition mechanism of coherence generation gamma photons by long-lived nuclear isomers in the single and two-quantum interaction with other species of excited radiators.

This method of recording of information affords the new perspectives in quantum cryptography and quantum information and has the tendency to improve the conception about quantum holograms observed in in literature [5, 7–9]. All these methods open new possibilities in the coding and decoding of data.

Author details

Nicolae A. Enaki
Quantum Optics and Kinetic Processes Lab, Institute of Applied Physics of Moldova, Chisinau, MD, Republic of Moldova

*Address all correspondence to: enakinicolae@yahoo.com

IntechOpen

References

[1] Collier R, Burckhardt C, Lin L. Optical Holography. New York: Academic Press, Inc.; 1971

[2] Bohm D. Quantum theory as an indication of a new order in physics-implicate and explicate order in physical law. Foundations of Physics. 1973;3(2): 139-168

[3] Talbot M. The Holographic Universe. New York: Harper-Collins Publishers, Inc.; 1991

[4] Gabor D. A new microscopic principle. Nature. 1948;161:777-778

[5] Abouraddy AF, Saleh BEA, Sergienko AV, Teich MC. Role of entanglement in two-photon imaging. Physical Review Letters. 2001;87(4):123602-123604

[6] Glauber RJ. Coherent and incoherent states of the radiation field. Physics Review. 1963;131(6):2766-2788

[7] Belinskii AV, Klyshko DN. Interference of light and Bell's theorem. Physics-Uspekhi. 1993;36(8):653-693

[8] Chrapkiewicz R, Jachura M, Banaszek K, Wasilewski W. Hologram of a single photon. Nature Photonics. 2016;10:576-579, arXiv preprint arXiv: 1509.02890

[9] Song X-B, Xu D-Q, Wang H-B, Xiong J, Zhang X, Cao D-Z, et al. Experimental observation of one-dimensional quantum holographic imaging. Applied Physics Letters. 2013; 103:131111. DOI: 10.1063/1.4822423

[10] Enaki NA, Ciornea VI. Enhanced generation rate of the coherent entanglement photon pairs in parametrical down conversion. Journal of Physics A: Mathematical and General. 2001;34:4601-4612

[11] Enaki N, Eremeev V. Two-photon lasing stimulated by collective modes.

Optics Communications. 2005;247: 381-392

[12] Enaki NA, Turcan M. Cooperative scattering effect between stokes and anti-stokes field stimulated by a stream of atoms. Optics Communications. 2012; 285(5):686-692

[13] Enaki NA. Chapter 2, Entanglement and cooperative effects between the mode components of Raman process in cavity and their analogy with atomic collective effects. In: Stewart N, editor. Book New Developments in Quantum Optics Research. NY, United States: Nova Science Publishers Inc; 2015. 133 p

[14] Palonpon AF, Ando J, Yamakoshi H, Dodo K, Sodeoka M, et al. Raman and SERS microscopy for molecular imaging of live cells. Nature Protocols. 2013;8: 677-692

[15] Yamakoshi H, Dodo K, Okada M, Ando J, Palonpon A, et al. Imaging of EdU, an alkyne-tagged cell proliferation probe, by Raman microscopy. Journal of the American Chemical Society. 2011; 133:6102-6105

[16] Gauthier DJ. Chapter 4 Two-photon lasers. Progress in Optics. 2003;45: 205-272

[17] Enaki NA. Mutual cooperative effects between single- and two-photon super-fluorescent processes through vacuum field. European Physical Journal D. 2012;66(4):21

[18] Enaki NA. Cooperative resonance interaction between one-and two-photon super-fluorescences trough the vacuum field. Journal of Physics Conference Series. 2012;338:012005

[19] Enaki NA. Non-Linear Cooperative Effects in Open Quantum Systems: Entanglement and Second Order

Coherence. NY, United States: Nova Science Publishers Inc; 2015. p. 355

[20] Boto AN, Kok P, Abrams DS, Braunstein SL, Williams CP, Dowling JP. Quantum interferometric optical lithography: Exploiting entanglement to beat the diffraction limit. Physical Review Letters. 2000;**85**(13):2733-2739

[21] Enaki NA. Superradiation from two-photon spontaneous decay. Journal of Experimental and Theoretical Physics. 1988;**67**:2033-2038 [(1988) Zh. Eksp. Teor. Fiz., 94, 135]

[22] Enaki N, Macovei M. Cooperative emission in the process of cascade and dipole-forbidden transitions. Physical Review A. 1997;**56**:3274-3286

[23] Enaki NA. Chapter 5: Peculiarities of two-photon holograms of nonlinear quantum optics and their connections with detection possibilities. In: Horizons in World Physics. Vol. 291. NY, USA: Nova Science Publishers; 2017. pp. 217-250

[24] Enaki NA. Chapter 2: Entanglement and cooperative effects between the mode components of Raman process in cavity and their analogy with atomic collective effects. In: New Developments in Quantum Optics Research. NY, USA: Nova Science Publishers Inc; 2015. pp. 51-97

[25] Dicke RH. Coherence in spontaneous radiation processes. Physics Review. 1954;**93**:99-110

[26] Brune M, Raimond JM, Haroche S. Theory of the Rydberg atom two-photon micromaser. Physical Review A. 1987;**35**:154-163

[27] Brune M, Raimond JM, Goy P, Davidovich L, Haroche S. Realization of a two-photon maser oscillator. Physical Review Letters. 1987;**59**:1899-1992

[28] Sorokin PP, Braslau N. Some theoretical aspects of a proposed double

quantum stimulated emission device. IBM Journal of Research and Development. 1964;**8**(2):177-181

[29] Prokhorov AM. Quantum electronics. Science. 1965;**10**:828

[30] Ali R, Ahmad I, Dunford RW, Gemmell DS, Jung M, Kanter EP, et al. Shape of the two-photon-continuum emission from the 1s-2s state in He-like krypton. Physical Review A. 1997;**55**: 994-1006

[31] Enaki N. Lithographic limit and problems of two-photon holograms in quantum optics. Proc. SPIE 7821, Advanced Topics in Optoelectronics, Microelectronics, and Nanotechnologies. 2010: 782104, 9 p. DOI: 10.1117/12. 882268

[32] Maimaiti A, Holzmann D, Truong VG, Ritsch H, Nic CS. Nonlinear force dependence on optically bound micro-particle arrays in the evanescent fields of fundamental and higher order microfibre modes. Scientific Reports. 2016;**6**:30131

[33] Saneh BEA, Teich MC. Fundameltals of Photonics. Wiley-Interscience; 2007. 947 pp

[34] Strekalov DV, Sergienko AV, Klyshko DN, Shih YH. Observation of two-photon "ghost" interference and diffraction. Physical Review Letters. 1995;**74**:3600

[35] Pittman TB, Shih YH, Strecalov DV, Sergienko AV. Optical imaging by means of two-photon quantum entanglement. Physical Review A. 1995; **52**:R3429

[36] Collins CB, Carroll JJ, Oganessian YT, Karamian SA. Evidence for K mixing in 178 Hf. Hyperfine Interactions. 1997;**107**:141-147